IMPROV-*ing*
AGILE TEAMS

IMPROV-*ing*
AGILE TEAMS

Using Constraints To Unlock Creativity

By Paul Goddard

Forewords by Liz Keogh and Neil Mullarkey

ABOUT THE AUTHOR

Paul Goddard is an established agile coach and trainer based in the United Kingdom. He has been assisting agile teams since 2003 and is a qualified Certified Scrum Trainer (CST) and Certified Scrum Coach (CSC). This book brings together two of his passions, coaching agile teams and improvisational theatre. The principles and practices are so closely linked, he uses them every day of his working and personal life. A regular speaker at agile conferences worldwide, Paul is also a long-standing member and contributor to the agile community in the UK and Europe. You can follow Paul on Twitter at @PaulKGoddard.

Edited by Rebecca T. Traeger

Design and Illustrations by Ole H. Størksen

Printed by Printech Solutions

Agilify Ltd., Bradford on Avon, UK
www.agilify.co.uk

Published 2015

ISBN 978-0-9933013-0-8

To Jocelyn and Owen,
the most creative little people I know.

As you get older, always try to make time for play.

Trust me, it will help.

Love, Daddy x

ACKNOWLEDGEMENTS

On Saturday, 15 March 2014, while walking through King's Cross, London, on a surprisingly sunny evening, I decided to write a book about two of my passions: coaching agile teams and improvisational theatre. I must thank the many people who have reviewed, questioned, edited, re-edited, listened, emailed, contributed, designed, and cajoled me and my book since that day.

A big thank you must go to anyone who was brave enough to attend one of my improv workshops or coaching sessions, even if you found yourself there without really knowing what you had let yourself in for. The games I selected for the book are largely down to those I have tried and tested on those willing to "give it a whirl". Those willing volunteers emerged from clients, conferences, and user groups alike, so without the agreeable nature of those people in the community much of the synergy between agile and improv would have been purely speculative.

Several pairs of agile eyes have scrutinised this book by volunteering to review chapters for me. Adam Weisbart, Tobias Mayer, Liz Keogh, Rob Cullingford, and Craig and Jen Livings all took time out of their busy schedules to read through my writing and give me much-needed feedback to improve. My editor, Rebecca Traeger, did an amazing job in making my writing much more coherent than its original form, and Ole H. Størksen brought this book to life with his illustrations and design prowess better than I ever could have imagined.

I do owe a huge debt of gratitude to Geoff Watts, who not only reviewed virtually the whole book for me and walked me through the book-writing process, but became accustomed to picking me up after I fell off the "writing wagon" numerous times.

In addition to the reviewers and expertise from the agile community, several members of the improv community were influential in assisting me to write this book. I have tried to credit any game or techniques I have used to the person responsible for its creation (or certainly for teaching it to me) but I recognise that, as the fundamentals of improv have existed in many different forms and adaptations for almost a century, the exact origins could be unintentionally misquoted.

Keith Johnstone was an inspiration to me, both from reading his books and also from attending his London workshop in September 2014. Despite his years, the energy and belief I witnessed in seeing Keith teach improvisation to students from any and all walks of life was eye-opening. Keith's work was a major realisation for me on the crossover of agile and improv, and I am still learning from his direction every day.

I enjoyed musing and working with several other teachers and improvisers while writing this book. Many thanks to Paul Z. Jackson, Paul Tevis, Jessica Litwak, John Webb, Laurence Saunders, Hilary Gallo, Lesley Adams, William Reay, Ian Coppinger, and all The Comedy Store Players, especially Lee Simpson, Richard Vranch, and Andy Smart. I reserve special thanks to Neil Mullarkey – firstly for being so open to sharing his wisdom based on 30 years of improvising but also for making me feel welcome at The Comedy Store in London whenever I attend.

To Sabrina, my wife, who has endured several nights when I couldn't sleep for thinking about this book.

To Owen, my son, whose smile can instantly turn an average day into a great day.

And to Jocelyn, my daughter, the source of all imaginative play that occurs in our house and so often the all-too-honest judge of my creative talent as a father.

As with improvisation itself, I couldn't have written this book alone, so to all of you – thank you.

CONTENTS

FOREWORD BY LIZ KEOGH

I first met Paul Goddard at Agile 2012 in Dallas, Texas. I was pretty exhausted at the time – too little sleep, too many people, too much excitement – and all I intended to do was find a seat somewhere to relax and take a break from the hectic sessions.

I passed a board where people could reserve breakout slots, and saw a card on it. One word caught my attention: "Improv". I thought of the television and radio shows. They were entertaining. They were relaxing. "That sounds like it might be fun," I thought. I wasn't expecting to actually join in.

Half an hour later, I was giggling with a small group of other trainees as we performed what seemed at the time to be ridiculous exercises. I remember trying to answer questions with other questions, astounded at how hard it seemed to be to avoid giving an answer. I remember saying "Yes, and…" and the difficulty of letting go of pre-conceived ideas to build on what others had said. I remember coming away challenged, but feeling relaxed nonetheless, as if something essential had been freed. I laughed, shook my head at the silliness, and walked away.

It was only later, while coaching, that I suddenly began to see the relevance.

I see it in the difference between teams that build on each other's successes, as opposed to those who tear each other down. I see it whenever I hear someone say "Yes, but…" and then watch the face of the person whose idea was just dismissed. I see it in the retrospectives of those who are just as keen to anchor the practices that are working as they are to improve the ones which aren't.

And then I saw it in myself. My coaching style became more positive, more supportive, and more prepared to listen to others. I also found that I was happier to play on my own strengths and rely on others to help.

The insight that Paul and other improv trainers have given me has been incredibly valuable to me throughout my journey, and I'm grateful to Paul for starting it off.

In this book, Paul has done more than just share his games and exercises. He also shares the reasons they work, and the joy they can bring. He shares direct comparisons between improv principles and agile practices. He shows in every chapter the real relevance of the art of improvisation to our daily work and lives. The insight that's been so valuable to me, and which I missed in such a startling fashion at the beginning, is written out in these pages.

Oh, yes, and…

…you can have it, too.

Liz Keogh is an independent Lean and Agile consultant based in London. She is a well-known blogger and international speaker, a core member of the BDD community and a contributor to a number of open-source projects including JBehave. She has a love of language, people and their potential, and creating choices, and is currently interested in modelling risk and change with complexity thinking and the Cynefin framework.

FOREWORD BY NEIL MULLARKEY

I first met Paul Goddard on Twitter, as you do these days. He loved improv and especially The Comedy Store Players, the ensemble I started along with Mike Myers and Paul Merton (among others) in 1985. Then he asked if I would run a workshop for him and his agile pals. I didn't know what agile was. I'm still not sure. I know it's used in software development. There are scrums and sprints. And even ScrumMasters. I had done a workshop for software people some years before. They told me that developers and testers might see themselves as different tribes. Testers were said to delight in finding a glitch that they could point out to developers. Agile seems to be about doing things more collaboratively and creatively, and realising that blueprints may not be much help but a continual process of prototyping really can be.

Paul is not the first person to see the connection between improv and business. Back when he was at the London Business School, I had conversations with Don Sull, an awfully clever professor of strategy now safely back at Harvard. He said, "I think improv is the answer. I'm just not sure what the question is." Don had looked at how improv-like techniques worked in developments in Formula 1, tactics for SAS/Navy SEALS and, um, software. His proposition was that you must not look too far ahead, that things are changing so quickly that a distant target would inevitably be superseded by the unpredictability of the world. I believe there is no area of business to which improv is not the answer – be it innovation, leadership, teamwork, strategy, negotiation, networking, presenting, recruitment, or what have you.

I learned a lot about agile that day I spent with Paul and his fellow coaches, who are eager to create a self-organising environment where decisions are taken fast and risks are encouraged but where everything can be used for learning, even the blind alleys. Paul has continued to delve since then to see how much his two interests have in common. He has watched many shows and attended workshops by teachers far better than I, and thought carefully about how improv principles apply to agile, and used exercises to make those applications work. He has emerged with five clear themes that will be of great value to the agile community. In doing so, he has also articulated why improv is such a potent force and has endured for nearly a century. The games at the end of each chapter will help you make sense of how creative – and enormously enjoyable – improv can be.

Improv is a mindset that means you can see another's point of view and are able to pursue it collaboratively, while not leaving yourself out of the equation. It gives a structure to creativity that is loose enough such that every "rule" can be toyed with so that the moment can live and context is king. To paraphrase Iain McGilchrist, author of *The Master and his Emissary* (which looks at the differences between the right and left hemispheres of the brain), if you privilege the left hemisphere, the danger is that you end up with answers that are completely rational but completely unreasonable. Or in the old days of software, a solution that solved a problem that was no longer relevant, or a solution that was actually more cumbersome than the problem. To innovate, people need both parts of the brain to be working together. Agile and improv share great left-brain approaches to liberating right-brain creativity. They are both about what actually works in practice.

So improv is the answer and, as the poet Rilke said, "Live the questions now. Perhaps you will then gradually, without noticing it, live along some distant day into the answer."[1]

Neil Mullarkey still performs with The Comedy Store Players in London every week unless he is off somewhere else teaching improv to help people in organisations develop their creative, communication, and leadership skills.

PREFACE

I firmly believe that the agile community can learn a great deal about our own application of agile from people working external to it. I wrote my book with the intention of informing you, the reader, of the benefit of combining agile theory with the mantra of improv theatre.

My intrigue with improv (largely the North American abbreviation) or impro (the label more common in the UK) came from frequenting a well-known comedy club in London, and watching in amazement at the ability of an improv troupe to embark on an uncertain journey with only an initial recommendation from the audience to aid them.

But we have to go back much further, to 1924 in Chicago, to really appreciate where improv began and how it became popular. Initially, young immigrant children were taught improv to help integrate them into the American way of life. The concept developed further over the next decade or two, to allow a wider range of people to hone their creativity and dramatic ability by playing one variety or another of the theatre game, which embraced the improv approach. Improv teaching continued to grow in Chicago over time, to a point where a pioneering improv acting company formed in 1955.[1]

Many of you may connect the word improv with comedy, with watching an improv group perform in front of an audience and (hopefully) making people laugh. The original improv comedy theatre academy and troupe grew from the aforementioned Chicago improv acting company. Iconic comedy and acting alumni of that improv comedy theatre academy include Dan Aykroyd, John Candy, Bill Murray, and Tina Fey.[2]

You might be more familiar with the TV adaptation of improv theatre. The typical TV form of improv will include a quick-fire type of improv game, where the group are limited by a random idea/location/character/emotion from the audience, and/or a type of rule or boundary for that particular game, which cannot be broken.

I became intrigued with how, within the boundary of a game, a great improv actor can captivate an audience for the duration of the whole performance. And with how an improv troupe can create an engaging and appealing narrative from virtually nothing. When I looked deeper, I learned that the *how* turned out to be the very place where the parallel between improv and agile can be found. (At the end of each chapter of my book, I have included an improv game – actually five of them – for you to try, with the hope that your team will learn how, too.)

When you think about it, an agile team can be limited in a related way – by their environment, their team make-up, the length of an iteration, or indeed the level of experience the team have in the product or methodology they follow. I have even heard people bad-mouth agile for being too mechanical and confined to technical delivery, or too overloaded with regimented ceremony to comprehend a larger, fuller horizon. People often fail to appreciate, however, that the very boundary around an agile team or framework can offer an opportunity for unbridled creativity.

Both agile development and improv can labour, too, under the fallacy that they are founded on wild and chaotic behaviour. The agile developer might be branded a cowboy coder, one who will do whatever, whenever, according to a whim. An improv actor might be relegated to being a bit of a clown, one who can only make it up "off the cuff" for a laugh. In truth, both agile and improv require a dedication to an unelaborate yet exacting framework and a team willing to firmly adhere to it in order to thrive.

I believe that a good agile approach will be one that (without reference to technology or context) will allow a team to embrace uncertainty and enjoy the freedom to explore their own creativity by collaborating frequently and effectively even under a time, requirement, or budgetary control.

Intended Audience

My book can benefit any individual or team looking to add more innovation and creative thought into their agile implementation. For the individual, an improv mode of thinking can be invigorating and motivating at work and in daily life. If, however, you are part of an agile team, or maybe have a duty to lead or teach an agile team, the improv approach defined in my book will help you appreciate how collaboration can be nurtured and developed purely by following and applying the guidance taught to many for nearly a century.

I have an expectation that you, the reader, have a fundamental knowledge of agile development, and I hope you believe that your team will benefit by adopting it wholeheartedly. I make no conjecture on which agile methodology, framework, or technique you have adopted.

Through my book, I hope to bring more creativity and imagination into a very technology-driven field. If I can convey even a minor percentage of the energy that I have for combining the nature of improv with the intricacy of commercial product development, then writing my book will have been a worthwhile adventure.

I would like to prove to you, the reader, that by following the five-principle approach provided in my book and applying an improv way of operating, your creativity capacity (and that of your team) can be unlocked and regularly improved, even within a controlled or limited working environment.

Do you accept my challenge?

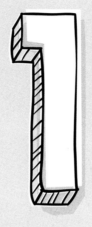

SAFETY

"We need somewhere to set our next scene," calls one of the two improvisers on stage to the audience. "A post office!" responds one of the audience members. A scene begins…

"Good morning, madam," says the first actor. The second actor stares back blankly, noticeably panicked and unable to respond.

The audience starts to move in their seats, feeling the awkwardness on stage. But then, the first actor rescues his partner from her stage fright by adding…

"Ah, Mrs Jefferson, sorry, I didn't recognise you there. Your throat must still be so sore after the operation…"

The actors and members of the audience breathe a collective sigh of relief and the scene continues…

SAFETY

The challenge of improvisational theatre is that the actors are thrust together on a stage in front of a paying audience, and are expected to entertain and engage that audience without a script. Given this, a natural human reaction would be one of fear – fear of an uncertain future, which a pre-written script cleverly avoids. Yet skilled improvisers thrive on that very uncertainty, engaging their audience within their emergent stories and taking the audience with them on their journey.

What is the foundation of their success?

Safety.

Improvisational theatre is at its best when the actors feel secure and safe with the other actors on stage. When actors feel unsure and unsafe, the result is often stage fright – that cringe-inducing moment when actors freeze on stage.

This chapter explores what a lack of safety can mean to software teams, how improvisational actors and groups work hard to establish a sense of safety, and how agile teams can increase trust and maximise success by establishing a secure environment from the very beginning.

The chapter ends, as does every chapter, with a number of improvisational games to play. This chapter's games are designed to help foster a safe team environment.

Lack of Trust

In a software team, lack of safety manifests itself in many different ways. In his book, *The Five Dysfunctions of a Team*, Patrick Lencioni examines the primary reasons why teams fail to work well together. Lencioni states that all of the dysfunctions listed in Figure 1.1 stem from a core "absence of trust" among the team members. Trust is the fundamental first step towards creating the safety that teams need to function effectively.

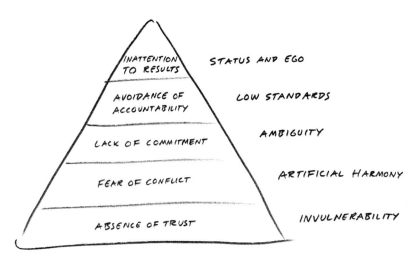

Figure 1.1 The underlying team dysfunction is an absence of trust

Lencioni describes the establishment of trust as "heavy lifting", the significant time and effort that is required from all the team members to build strong foundations for the team.[1] **Teams need a foundation of trust so that they can support each other in times of crisis, as well as disagree without prejudice to help find alternative solutions.** Without this trust, crisis and disagreement can destroy a team. Newly formed teams are particularly susceptible to trust issues because team members tend to be hesitant to show weakness, often out of a fear of seeming inferior to their new teammates. This has a snowball effect, because when certain team members *appear* infallible, others are less likely to offer support.

Consequently, these team members tend to work alone more often, which could actually make them feel more isolated and *less* safe. On the other hand, if a few team members are willing to accept and show their vulnerabilities, it can help others feel safer in sharing their weak points too. When this happens, teams begin to learn how to support each other.

Trust between team members is essential, whether you are building software or creating unscripted stories on stage. Improvisers on stage have learned the hard way that a scene will not work unless they work together as a team. They know that it is much more difficult for one individual to create an interesting scene alone, so they rely on each other to add colour and keep the action moving forward. Therefore, they purposefully develop trust so that they increase their chances of success. This trust is reinforced in the form of rescue, which was illustrated in the scenario that opened this chapter. Should an improviser freeze on stage or struggle for direction or inspiration, fellow improvisers will come to their aid by adding extra lines or by physically jumping into the scene. **Rescuing each other is a great way to establish trust among teammates, but in order to be rescued, individual team members must be prepared to show their weaknesses or flaws.**

> *"As long as you are on stage with people you trust,*
> *then there is nothing to fear"*
> Richard Vranch[2]

Software teams might not be as acutely aware of their need for trust as improvisers are. Some teams develop trust slowly and organically over time, by getting to know one another and discovering each other's strengths and weaknesses during the highs and lows of working together on various projects. However, if those teams actively worked to establish trust during their infancy, they could be more trusting – and possibly more successful – much earlier.

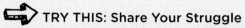 **TRY THIS: Share Your Struggle**
Admit to some part of your role where you struggle.
Share that weakness with a member of your team and
ask for help with improving it.

Fear of Failure

> *"I have not failed.*
> *I've just found 10,000 ways that won't work."*
> Thomas Edison[3]

Like many inventors, Thomas Edison knew that innovative solutions are often born from failed attempts. In fact, many great advances and iconic product discoveries have been the unexpected results of failed experiments. Coca-Cola was discovered by a pharmacist who, while looking for a cure for headaches, realised that his mixture of ingredients actually tasted quite pleasant. Penicillin was only discovered when Alexander Fleming analysed how bacteria had formed in a Petri dish left next to an open window. Scientists at 3M were in fact attempting to make a super-adhesive when they found they had created the exact opposite – the Post-it note, a product that did not stick very well. Post-its, the mainstay of many agile teams, would have never been sold on the market if one of the scientists, Art Fry, had not realised that the notes made for perfect bookmarks in his hymnal because they left no residue once removed.[4]

Sometimes when people try new things, they fail to achieve their goals or just get it wrong. When individuals feel safe to explore new ideas within a team, this failure is no big deal. If, on the other hand, failure doesn't seem acceptable to a team, people might react instinctively by making excuses, hiding their struggles, or even actively covering up their shortcomings. I can remember a good example of this from one of my first agile teams. During one iteration, I noticed that one of my colleagues was repeating the same update each day in the daily stand-up. He never seemed to move on to new tasks or discover new information. When I later discussed this one-on-one with the developer in question, he admitted that he was in fact struggling with understanding some legacy code but didn't want to admit to his peers that he needed help, for fear of looking inferior.

Why do so many software teams tend to view failure so negatively? One reason is that in this rapidly changing industry, deadlines and budgets are typically set against a team's ability to overcome a challenge in the shortest time possible, for the least cost. When businesses leave no margin for error or indeed failure, trust and safety suffer.

Intolerance for failure isn't unique to the software industry, though. Punishing failure is part of most people's schooling. The education system in itself is based on 19th-century thinking for an industrial age. Schoolchildren have always been judged on individual ability and instructed that in order to achieve in life, you need a strong understanding in logical subjects such as mathematics and science, as opposed to more creative subjects like music and drama. Mathematics and science are subjects that are easily assessed by a student's ability to find "the right answer", so individuals learn from an early age that success depends on being right. Furthermore, the students who excel at finding the right answer in these subjects tend to gain higher grades and pursue further education or (maybe) get a better job than those who don't.[5]

In the UK, the pressure of academic study increases over time and usually culminates when students reach the age of 16. At that time, students are given various exams or tests in which they are expected to demonstrate the knowledge and acumen they have digested over several years of teaching. While some students can cope with that pressure, others struggle with the fear of failing.

Individuals, it seems, have grown up in a world where the right answer is rewarded, more so than the steps they have taken to arrive at that answer. Is it any wonder that failure is viewed so negatively in the workplace?

Making Failure Acceptable

Conversely, improvisers thrive on failure – some of the games they play actively *encourage* it. The actors on stage trust each other implicitly and graciously accept whatever lines are spoken. There are no wrong or stupid suggestions. The audience enjoys the tangles the improvisers get into from some of the unexpected lines, and laugh and cheer at the so-called failures that occur. Those reactions encourage the improvisers and help them feel safe, the same way that a waiter who drops a tray full of glasses might feel less clumsy when the restaurant's customers joyfully cheer at the incident. Short-form improvisation (the games on TV programmes such as *Whose Line Is It Anyway?*) deliberately uses failure as a device to create flow and energy. Changing the scene or changing the actors on stage mid-stream doesn't mean that things aren't going well; instead, it's part of the game – a part that is designed to temporarily disrupt the rhythm and scene the actors have established to spark their creativity.[6]

> *"Mistakes are where the gold is."*
> Richard Vranch[7]

Agile teams also can benefit from practising failure, learning how to cope with it and how to benefit from it. The games and exercises in this chapter aim to help teams go through that process. **When teams begin to believe that failure is acceptable and can even have a positive outcome, such as learning new ideas or trying other solutions, it opens the door to creativity.**

 TRY THIS: One Failure, Five Positives
Cast your mind back to a time where you or your team experienced failure. Try to extract five different positives that came from it. Even the smallest positives can help make failure seem less painful next time.

Finding Your Flow

In professional sports, peak physical conditioning is almost a given. During his 2014 seminar, sports performance coach Andy McCann explained that there is very little difference among the elite athletes when it comes to athletic ability – the difference between a gold and silver medal at an Olympic final can come down to hundredths of a second. According to McCann, the current thinking among sports psychologists is that the marginal gains required by today's top-level athletes stem more from mental toughness than from more demanding training regimes. Mental toughness is the ability to remain completely focused in high-pressure situations, so much so that nothing can distract you from the goal.[8]

According to Wikipedia, psychologist Mihály Csíkszentmihályi postulated that we are motivated as individuals when we achieve flow. This is the state that athletes refer to as "in the zone", where they are almost oblivious to anything other than the tasks in hand. A variation of Csíkszentmihályi's Flow Model is shown in Figure 1.2.

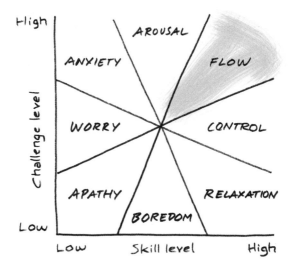

Figure 1.2: The Flow Model[9]

As Figure 1.2 illustrates, flow theory postulates that flow occurs where a high challenge level matches an equally high skill level, whereby individuals have confidence in their ability to complete the task at hand. This diagram also shows that undertaking a challenge beyond a person's skill level can increase anxiety, and by the same token, that challenges well below a person's skill level can lead to apathy.

Often in software teams, managers continually exhort developers to "do their best" or "go the extra mile" to make the delivery a success. I've rarely seen this help; in fact, it seems only to add to the pressure and expectations developers and agile teams already feel. Yet leadership wonders why teams sometimes "drop the ball" or become anxious when they are asked to achieve stretch goals. I believe that while software organisations continually push towards stretch goals or minimal cycle time, agile teams will continue to flounder or freeze, or worse still, cut quality to meet unrealistic deadlines.

> *"You can't be safe if you are trying your best"*
> Keith Johnstone[10]

When I first heard this Johnstone quote, I thought it seemed somewhat contradictory and counter-intuitive. Yet upon reflection, I realised that his point is a valid one. People put extra pressure on themselves when they are trying to work beyond their skill levels, thereby moving into the anxiety state within the flow model. Anxiety can cause individuals to freeze and slow their natural responses. For improvisers, trying too hard for a laugh leads to selfish behaviour on stage, where actors become individuals looking for personal success rather than teammates supporting their fellow actors on stage. Similarly, when agile teams and developers are under strain to go beyond their capacity or remit, self-preservation kicks in; people will take care of themselves rather than each other. This makes for a tense, fear-driven working environment where team members rarely feel safe.

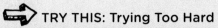 **TRY THIS: Trying Too Hard**

Can you think of a recent situation where members of your team have pushed themselves beyond their limits or capacity? What were the consequences?

Slowing Down

When individuals are in a situation that makes them feel unsafe, such as public speaking engagements or performances, they often rush to get it over with as quickly as possible. Novice improvisers sometimes demonstrate this human tendency on stage by speaking and moving too quickly, thereby leaving the audience confused and disengaged.

The software industry has become obsessed by speed and time to market. I believe this amplifies a fear of failure, as it is no longer acceptable to slow down. The advice I was given throughout my life in stressful situations is to *s l o w d o w n* and take a breath. I now make a conscious effort to talk more slowly than normal when I am speaking in public, for instance. Some of the problems I see when I teach teams or coach organisations stem from people trying to do too much work, too fast. The cost of failure rises with the amount of work in progress, which is why teams are petrified of estimating projects inaccurately and of missing overly ambitious deadlines.

Mike Cohn also hints at this with his "Primary Criticism of Scrum" blog post, namely that teams have become too focused on finishing the work and "getting things done", rather than using a longer sprint length to experiment with different ideas before deciding on the most appropriate solution. As a result, two-week sprints have become far more commonplace than the original 30-day concept that Ken Schwaber originally insisted on. While there are many benefits to shorter sprints, the downside to shorter sprints is that it is harder for a team to justify time to explore options before they decide on how to implement a solution.[11] In *Agile Software Development with Scrum*, Schwaber and Beedle refer to Scrum teams as "hotbeds of creativity",[12] which is something I sadly see lacking in many of the teams I work with, mainly due to those teams being focused more on delivery than innovation.

> "We cannot solve our problems with the same thinking
> we used when we created them."
> Albert Einstein[13]

In his book, *Hare Brain, Tortoise Mind,* Guy Claxton describes how the mind has three different processing speeds. The first (and quickest) is faster than thought itself – our instinctive reflexes or reactions. People commonly refer to these as their wits (having their wits about them). The second, much slower speed is logical thought. This involves using intelligence to work things out, given that there is a logical solution to find. Individuals apply this processing speed when they take exams, fix a broken car engine, or even plan their next summer holiday. Claxton refers to this mode as "d-mode", meaning default or indeed deliberation mode. People who are good at solving these types of problems are considered bright or clever.

But underneath the d-mode of intelligence, the brain processes at an even slower speed. This mental register is often less purposeful or logical, and is more playful or even dream-like. This is why people can sometimes come up with great new ideas in the most odd scenarios or situations, such as driving alone on a long car journey or lying in a hot bath. Claxton's research now convincingly shows that slower, less deliberate modes of mind are particularly suited to making sense of situations that are intricate, shadowy, or ill-defined. This third type of intelligence is often called creativity or even wisdom.

Claxton's observation is that the modern Western world has marginalised this third type of mindfulness as lazy or merely recreational; only active deliberation is seen as productive.[14] The software organisations that I have worked within seem to mirror that observation; however, so many of the macro-level issues that software companies discover are rooted in complex human behaviours, which the logical d-mode approach will struggle to solve with its logical, predictive thinking.

In the modern technology-driven world, organisations have become overly time-conscious and obsessed by efficiency. The fear of being surpassed in the market by a competitor forces us to focus purely on speed rather than creativity. People rarely allow any time for the "luxury" of just thinking – they don't feel safe if they aren't delivering – which I believe causes teams to miss out on some truly innovative solutions.

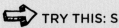 **TRY THIS: Slow Your Mind**

Identify the times and places when your "slowest" thinking occurs. This could be in the shower, just before you go to sleep, or driving on a long journey. How could you introduce this state of mind into a working environment?

Not Advancing

In improvisational theatre, Keith Johnstone constructs games to teach students how to slow down on stage. He refers to this as "not advancing".[15] Slowing down gives a richer, deeper performance on stage and on screen as well. Stars of silent movies are perhaps the best examples of how slowing down makes a film scene more interesting, as they couldn't rely on speech to add realism to the scene. Charlie Chaplin, for example, could make *not* falling down a manhole look interesting for 30 seconds, which seems like a lifetime for such a simple act.[16]

When student actors are going too fast in a scene, Johnstone tells them to pause at the point when they need to speak and rephrase what they are about to say into a different line in their heads, before then saying that new line out loud. While this breaks the flow of conversation slightly, and might make the actors briefly look less intelligent, strangely they often are better actors purely because they have slowed down. In other words, giving the improvisers permission to pause and consider before acting on an impulse makes for a richer performance.

Agile teams are largely unaware of the benefits of not advancing an activity. I recently asked a team I was coaching to imagine the slowest possible way they could fix a high-priority defect. While the initial response was one of bewilderment, what emerged was actually a higher-quality process than the one that the team was currently following. This team went on to formally publicise their slow version as what would constitute a "good defect fix", a process that included test automation, code review, and refactoring of legacy code. They were genuinely amazed at how much their defect-fixing process improved as a result of having explicit permission to consider a slower fix rather than a quicker one.

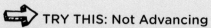 **TRY THIS: Not Advancing**

Choose a trivial, simple, quick everyday task such
as preparing to sit down at a desk, checking your
appearance in a mirror before you leave the house, or
putting on a pair of shoes, and try to slow the task down.
What improvements come to mind as you purposefully
consider each step of the task?

Playing at Work, Working at Play

For agile teams, a safe environment starts with a team that trusts each other enough to make mistakes, to work as a team, and to take the time to slow down and implement better solutions. This safe environment, though, is only as good as the degree to which their employers support and reinforce that level of safety.

Improvisers refer to themselves and each other as *players*. Individuals feel safe when they feel like things are just pretend – when it isn't so serious, when it doesn't count, when it doesn't matter if they win or lose. Work, however, is different. Work tends to be about winning, about doing things right the first time. When people are in a work mindset, they stop playing and get serious. When this happens, they also block innovative ideas.

In order to access their own creativity, agile teams need the space to play. Whether you are an agile practitioner, facilitator, coach, manager, or trainer, your focus should be on making it safe for others to play, because only then can they start to exercise their more creative selves. Sometimes people just need permission to let go.

What can you do today to help your team to play more?

IMPROVISATION GAMES

Each chapter in this book contains several short-form improvisation games that I have either learned, adapted, or created for you to try with your own agile team. Each game description includes a short **synopsis** of the game, a sample **script** for the facilitator, ideas for **side coaching**, opportunities for a **shift** in emphasis, topics for group **speculation** and contemplation, and **suggestions** for alternatives.

Every game also has a quick-reference guide with the following information:

- optimal number of **players**, typically expressed as a range;
- approximate **time** and **energy level** required;
- whether the game is more suited for **individual** or **team** development;
- how far the game might stretch the players' **visual**, **verbal**, and **physical** talents; and
- scenarios in which the game might be useful, specifically agile meetings or ceremonies.

Many of these characteristics are rated on a scale of 1 to 5 stars, where 1 is *least* and 5 is *most*. You will find this guide as a table at the beginning of each game.

PLAY
SAFETY
GAMES

Safety Games

The games in this chapter aim to help establish trust between team members by learning to play with failure, rescuing each other and building a safer environment.

ANYONE WHO?[17]

Players	Timebox	Energy Level	Individual	Team	Visual	Verbal	Physical	Scenario
7±2	10 mins	*****	**	****	***	****	****	Team Building, Retro-spective

Synopsis

This game encourages players to expose some facts about themselves, which may uncover some similarities with other players. Exposing truths about themselves increases players' vulnerability. This game also encourages players to rescue each other, which helps to build trust.

Script

The facilitator of the game should arrange chairs in a circle. All players sit on the chairs and the facilitator stands in the centre of the circle.

FACILITATOR: "The person in the centre of this circle will tell us something about themselves by starting a statement with 'Anyone who...' If you share that fact with the person in the middle, you must stand up and find a new seat. The person in the middle should sit in one of the vacated seats."

Some examples, assuming the person in the centre has these characteristics, could be:

- anyone who has red hair;
- anyone who had eggs for breakfast;
- anyone who has children; or
- anyone who is wearing shoes.

As there will always be one more person than the number of seats, one of the players will always be left standing.

FACILITATOR: "Now there is a new person in the middle of the circle. Try another 'Anyone who…' and find a new seat…"

Side Coaching

While the game is underway, if players are struggling to think of ideas, interject when appropriate with "Look around the circle for inspiration!"

Should the question result in no one standing up, ask the central player to think of an alternative question.

Speculation

"How did it feel being in the middle? Why?"

"How did it feel watching people in the middle?"

"What made the game enjoyable?"

"Did any questions make you feel awkward?"

"What did we learn about each other during this game?"

Suggestions

In a retrospective, use this game to encourage players to admit their struggles in the previous iteration. For instance, "Anyone who broke something in the last iteration?" or "Anyone who was late for a meeting in the last iteration?" If the team can accept these vulnerabilities, they might be more prepared to discuss how to address them together.

DAILY "TAND-UP"[18]

Players	Timebox	Energy Level	Individual	Team	Visual	Verbal	Physical	Scenario
7±2	15 mins	**	*****	***	*	*****	*	Daily Stand-up

Synopsis

The constraint in this game is to talk without using the letter S. This game is difficult by design, but when players understand it's acceptable to make mistakes, the game flows more quickly and becomes more fun and energetic. Other players also listen more closely, as they are trying to catch their fellow players out.

Script

Stand in a circle, with all players facing each other.

FACILITATOR: "We are going to try and run today's stand-up without using the letter S. If you slip up, you have to hand over to the next person to carry on, and wait until it's your turn again…"

Encourage other players to listen for the letter and point out when the rule is broken.

Continue around the circle until the appropriate questions have been answered and the daily stand-up has concluded.

Shift

If the dialogue is slow and stilted, explain to players that it's OK to fail at this game. In fact, failing quickly allows the other players to get back in the game.

Speculation

"What made the game quicker?"

"What slowed the game down?"

"What made the game more fun?"

"What did we learn here about 'failure'?"

Suggestions

Try the game with a different letter such as *b*, *f*, or *p*. Stay clear of vowels, as this makes the game almost impossible.

Try using whole words instead of just a letter. Good examples are *done*, *blocked*, or *tested*, or you could always ask the team for some suggestions.

ONE VOICE[19]

Players	Timebox	Energy Level	Individual	Team	Visual	Verbal	Physical	Scenario
7±2	15 mins	**	***	****	*	*****	*	Daily Stand-up, Estimation

Synopsis

This game encourages small groups of players to speak together in unison so that the team can build safety in numbers. Agile teams can ask pairs of players to speak together at a daily stand-up or during an estimation session. (This is quite a fun game to try in a non-work context as well.)

Script

Standing is best for this game. Divide the group into smaller groups of two to three players.

FACILITATOR: "In your groups, you may only answer questions by speaking in unison. If we can't understand you, you will have to work together to make your response more coherent."

Try everyday conversation, just to warm the groups up.

FACILITATOR: "Hi. How are you doing today?"

Expect the groups to respond in a disjointed fashion. Ask them to repeat themselves until they have delivered a united response. Once the groups understand how the game works, you can have them respond in the context of the meeting.

For example, in a daily stand-up, ask the groups to describe what they achieved yesterday, what they plan to do today, and what's stopping them.

For estimation sessions, ask groups to agree on estimates by looking at each other and sounding out the estimate very slowly, starting with the words "We think the estimate is…" and then working together to choose a number, for example "thfthffffffff-iiii-vv-e". Given a hesitant or completely incoherent response, the facilitator should follow up with some clarifying questions and repeat the exercise until a more natural and agreeable estimate is spoken.

Side Coaching

"Try not to lead too much. If you notice you are, try to step back."

"If you find yourself just following other players, try to take a little more control."

Don't be shy in asking the players to repeat themselves. If a response is incoherent, chime in with "Sorry, I don't understand. Can you say that again?"

Speculation

"What skills were you using to find agreement on what to say?"

"Did any of you find others leading the conversation?"

"Did any of you find yourself following others more?"

"What did you change when your response wasn't understood?"

COLOMBIAN HYPNOSIS[20]

Players	Timebox	Energy Level	Individual	Team	Visual	Verbal	Physical	Scenario
4–16	10 mins	****	****	**	*	*	*****	Anytime

Synopsis

This game establishes trust between two people. Using only one finger, one player will lead another player, whose eyes are closed, around the room.

Script

Ask the players to form pairs.

FACILITATOR: "One of you will be the leader, and one of you will be the follower."

Give the pairs a chance to agree to those roles.

FACILITATOR: "Now both players hold out one index finger, and allow your finger to touch the other player's finger at the end. Once contact has been made, the followers must close their eyes as if under hypnosis. The role of the leaders is to guide the followers around the room, avoiding objects and furniture they might encounter."

By varying the pressure and direction of just the index finger, it is possible to lead the follower around the room without harm or injury, if the followers are willing to trust their fellow players.

Side Coaching

"Focus on the contact your finger has made…"

"Trust your partners to look after you and follow their lead…"

Speculation

"How did it feel to close your eyes and trust your partner's commands?"

"How did you establish that trust between you?"

"Did anything challenge or break that trust?"

Suggestions

It is possible to use this technique to climb over or under tables, sit down on chairs, or lie on the floor.

If players are uncomfortable with body contact between players, you can try the same game with players holding a pen or pencil at both ends.

PSYCHIC STAND-UP

Players	Timebox	Energy Level	Individual	Team	Visual	Verbal	Physical	Scenario
7±2	15 mins	*	****	****	*	*****	*	Daily Stand-up

Synopsis

Players deliver their updates on behalf of others in the group, based on their intuition and an apparent psychic ability to predict what other team members will be working on today. This game hints at how safe the players feel as they suggest what other players should be committing to each day.

Script

FACILITATOR: "In today's stand-up, you will give your update on behalf of another attendee. The same three questions apply, but you will answer with what *they* did yesterday, what *they* will do today, and what is blocking *them*."

Allow the first player the chance to choose the person whose update will be predicted. When the first player is finished speaking, the psychic ability then passes on to the chosen one, and that player then gives the next update for another player in the group.

Continue this until all the fortunes have been read and the team has synchronised the day's work.

Speculation

"What made it easier to predict someone's future?"

"How did it feel when someone told you what you were doing?"

"What caused you to feel safe or unsafe in that exercise?"

Suggestions

Play with the questions: "What caused them pain yesterday?" or "Where will they be lucky today?"

Encourage the players to act like mind readers and have some fun making bold predictions!

SPONTANEITY

Two improvisers are on stage. "Can you suggest a profession for us to share?"
one of the actors asks the audience. "Plumbers!" responds an eager member
of the crowd. Without missing a beat, the first actor holds out an open hand
to his acting partner and asks, "Can you pass me the snake?"

The other improviser looks confused. Why is a plumber asking for a snake?
What does a snake have to do with being a plumber? What this improviser
doesn't know is that in plumbing terms, a snake is a long, thin, flexible rod
used for unblocking pipes.

An awkward silence falls on the theatre as the scene momentarily stalls.
Both actors on stage begin to look unsure as to what to do or say next.

"There are snakes in here? Argh! Quick, climb up on top of the bath!"
exclaims the second actor. In response, the first actor immediately leaps
up and begins to climb.

The scene now unfolds as two plumbers try to escape from a bathroom
full of poisonous snakes…

SPONTANEITY

*"The fun stuff comes when someone is not so strict on
sticking to the script. You're allowed the spontaneity,
and great moments can happen."*
Jennifer Aniston[1]

In simple terms, improvisational theatre is the art of creating change spontaneously while on stage. There is no set script – the actors make it up as they go along, creating a twisting, evolving story that, ideally, elicits an audience's engagement. Yet improvisers have to work hard to unlock and indeed maintain their creative edge. To do this, they practise a simple protocol that all of the actors respect and understand. More specifically, the actors follow a framework built around offers and blocks that helps them to create and adapt without hesitation.

This framework, and the spontaneity required to make it work effectively, is not specific to the stage – it also applies to the way we operate and collaborate at work, and even in our personal lives. The agile manifesto states, "We have come to value … responding to change over following a plan."[2] In other words, change is inevitable in the software world, so people should find ways to allow teams to thrive in a change-filled environment.

This chapter explores the concept of spontaneity, how improvisers are able to create and develop stories and scenes spontaneously, and how agile teams can learn to improve spontaneity and openness to new ideas in order to increase their own creativity.

Spontaneity: Good or Bad?

Being spontaneous means different things to different people. Google first defines the adjective as follows:

1. "performed or occurring as a result of a sudden impulse or inclination and without premeditation or external stimulus."

I can see how this kind of spontaneity could be construed as a risky approach in business. In business, acting without thinking things through first could be considered as wasteful, chaotic, and hugely unnerving for all those involved. A spontaneous CEO of a company could be judged as impulsive and rash, lacking strategy and direction. Yet in improvisation and indeed in life, spontaneity is the key to creativity. Interestingly, Google's second definition seems to have a much more positive spin:

2. "having an open, natural, and uninhibited manner."[3]

This definition fits the profile of the ideal improviser, someone who consistently produces results in the midst of uncertainty, and seems much more palatable to a business culture as well. However, in this chapter I will explore how both definitions can be appropriate and indeed beneficial to agile teams.

Child's Mind

To help me explain child's mind, I need to tell you about my five-year-old daughter, whom I like to think of as my own (adorable) creative consultant. Jocelyn is quite possibly the most spontaneous human being I know. As a toddler, Jocelyn would, at times and without prompting, decide to draw a flower on the dining room table, using a Sharpie. At other times, she would take all the saucepans and tins out of the kitchen cupboards and hide them around the house. She also seemed to love a game I called *Find Daddy's Credit Cards* – it was one of her favourites and usually lasted for several days.

When I asked Jocelyn why she did those "naughty" things, she would describe to me in great detail the game or story that she had invented. Limits, such as our rules and frustration, didn't enter her mind – to her, the props she used merely added to the realism of her adventures. For Jocelyn, this was imaginative play. For me as a parent, this was an exhausting effort. I dealt with it by shutting down her games and asking her, in essence, to refrain from such spontaneous displays of creativity. My instinct was to add a control to relieve my frustration, rather than encourage her spontaneous nature.

As people go through life, their parents, teachers, colleagues, and managers impose similar controls and conformity on their actions. As such, most individuals associate acts of spontaneity with getting into trouble. If people succumb to this notion, however, they will suppress their innate curiosity, creativity, and sense of adventure – their child's mind. The agile manifesto calls us to remember the power of spontaneity when it suggests "individuals and interactions over process and tools".[4] In other words, when processes and tools dominate the organisational culture, then agility, spontaneity, and creativity take a back seat. As Jocelyn gets older, I still want her to enjoy the creative freedom she gets from her spontaneous imagination. So she now has a drawer full of washable markers she can access rather than my Sharpies, and a stack of expired credit cards that she uses to create her imaginary shopping trips with her baby dolls. These are the tools I created to make spontaneity acceptable as a creative activity, rather than rash and wasteful behaviour.

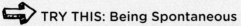 **TRY THIS: Being Spontaneous**

Recall a recent decision or event (work or personal) that occurred without premeditation. What emotions are stimulated as a result?

Untraining the Brain

During some of my own agile improv workshops, I will run a game called What's in the Box? to help people rediscover the spontaneity that comes so naturally to my daughter. During the game, players will mime taking objects out of an imaginary box, a box that can contain anything they want it to. During a recent event, I was demonstrating the game with a volunteer to the rest of the class:

ME: "What's in the box?"

VOLUNTEER: "Er... er..." There is an obvious pause while he filters something. "A grape."

ME: "Really? Did you start to say something else?"

VOLUNTEER: "Yes."

ME: "What did you think of first?"

VOLUNTEER: "A plum."

ME: "Why didn't you say plum?"

VOLUNTEER: "Well, there are ladies present!"

In this example, the volunteer had screened the word *plum* as it was analogous to a man's testicle; he thought that others might consider that word rude or offensive. **People's imagination and free thought often is slowed by subconscious screening of their ideas.** Johnstone teaches his improv students that imagination is suppressed in three different ways:

1. Psychotic Thought

Individuals sometimes reject their own idea because they fear they will be labelled *mad*. A child who believes that monsters really do live in the wardrobe is cute, yet an adult who believes the same is considered insane. In a professional context, suggesting ideas that are considered mad could be seen as wasteful. Sometimes simply asking the question "What would make this situation even worse?" can help people unload all of their ideas, even the off-kilter ones. Their focus can then switch to examining these ideas to see if they could be used for positive effect.

2. Obscene Thought

Individuals also reject ideas that could offend others. Obscenity, however, is highly subjective. Some individuals might find select words obscene; at the same time, some organisations might be offended by certain concepts or terms that they deem unacceptable, such as failure or self-managing teams.

For this reason, on occasion it might be necessary for a team to sit down and define what offends the team members within a team. In one coaching engagement, I worked with a team that was experiencing a lot of frustration with a particularly fragile product, riddled with errors and issues. I asked a team to sit down during a retrospective and write down all the offensive words they would use to describe the product without filtering their language. Once all these words had been written on cards (anonymously) we displayed them all on the table, and I asked everyone to remove words that offended them. This gave any member of the group a chance to outlaw certain words without anyone having to discuss or even verbalise them. As a result, the group members learned which adjectives were acceptable to the group's discussions and which were not. Knowing which terms are acceptable and which are not can help alleviate people's concerns and free their minds.

3. Unoriginal Thought

Individuals often block their imaginations when they feel unoriginal. People will search harder for an idea when they want to be thought of as clever and inventive. They might believe this gets them noticed, but what it actually does is slow the idea-creation process by skipping over more simple and common-sense approaches.[5]

By addressing these filters directly, teams can start to engage their creative minds in a more spontaneous way.

When I am coaching, I bypass the psychotic and obscene filters by asking the team to pretend to be a famous person or character that might ignore those filters. During a retrospective at Nokia, for example, we had just been through a particularly unpleasant sprint, laden with delays and issues. Yet at the retrospective, when I asked the question "What made you angry during the sprint?", I was met with a subdued and apathetic response. So I quickly rephrased the question…

"What would Dr. Evil say about this sprint?"

By doing this, I gave permission for the team to think and speak in the guise of a movie character (portrayed by Mike Myers, in the hugely successful Austin Powers movies) who was borderline insane. Only then did people relax the mad and obscene filters enough to verbalise all the terrible things that had happened during the sprint. Once the problems were out in the open, we could start to talk more actively about how to correct them.

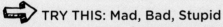 **TRY THIS: Mad, Bad, Stupid**
Ask team members for suggestions of fictional characters who would fall into the categories of being mad, bad, or stupid. When the team needs help to find a solution, ask them what those characters would do in a similar situation.

Hats and Masks

"Masks have more ideas than people do"
Charlie Chaplin[6]

When I am trying to encourage a team to loosen their filters and use their imaginations more freely, I will occasionally invite the use of hats and masks. This is usually met with trepidation initially, but every team I have tried this with soon becomes completely absorbed in the theatre of the exercise. **Hats, masks, and even costumes can help people access their ideas more readily because they help individuals feel as if they are thinking like other people.** Even Charlie Chaplin needed help relaxing his filters; his character and mannerisms only came to him when he tried on his trademark outfit and iconic moustache for the first time.[7]

The idea of using hats and masks is similar to Edward de Bono's "Six Thinking Hats", where a team collectively wears a series of metaphorical hats, each coloured and attached to a distinct thought process.[8] However, physical hats are much more fun! So instead of asking the team to put on an imaginary white hat of discovery to gather information, why not ask them to actually don an actual deerstalker and study the facts like Sherlock Holmes?

I have run some truly inspiring workshops with attendees wearing police officers' helmets, builders' hard hats, balaclavas, and masks of the Simpsons and other cartoon characters.

When a person puts on a hat or a mask, that person becomes someone else, and the responsibility for being creative is momentarily passed on to that character.

Playing a role prevents people from filtering unoriginal thoughts and allows them to focus on being more obvious. Ideas will flow more quickly as a result. In these examples, my role as facilitator was to enable the spontaneity of the group members by removing the brain's filters, albeit temporarily, in a relaxed (and safe) team setting. Improvisers focus on increasing the spontaneity of their fellow actors on stage by creating an open mode to work in, fuelled by positive suggestions. The next section takes a closer look at how they do that.

TRY THIS: Wear the Hat
Imagine yourself walking through an enormous store, filled with every type of hat you can think of. What style of hat would you choose to try on? What would your character then say in the mirror?

Offers

The basic unit of currency in improvisational theatre is an **offer**. Offers can be physical or verbal prompts, words, or lines that invite other actors on stage to continue the action.[9] For example, in a typical improv scene, two actors stand on stage together and ask the audience to suggest a setting where two people may meet. Suppose the audience's suggestion is "coffee shop".

Given only the location of the scene to start with, the two actors must exchange offers to allow the scene to progress and hopefully remain interesting to the audience.

First Actor: "Good morning, sir…"

This is a good initial offer. In just three words, the first actor has suggested two elements of the scene – the time of day and the second actor's role as a customer. A good offer is an obvious one. The second actor can now respond:

Second Actor: "Good morning. Large cappuccino to go, please."

Another good offer. The second actor has confirmed the first actor's offer, in effect saying, "*Yes*. It is morning and I am a customer." The second actor has also extended his own offer, effectively communicating, "*And*, I suggest you play the role of a barista."

In two short phrases, both actors have established a mutual understanding and the basis of a scene to work from. This is the *Yes, And* protocol, and is the primary one used by improvisation actors. The default for these actors is that everything and anything they offer will be accepted by their partners. In this example, each actor is enabling the other to thrive. This puts both actors at ease and makes them feel safer in the scene, allowing collaboration to flow more easily so that an interesting storyline can emerge.

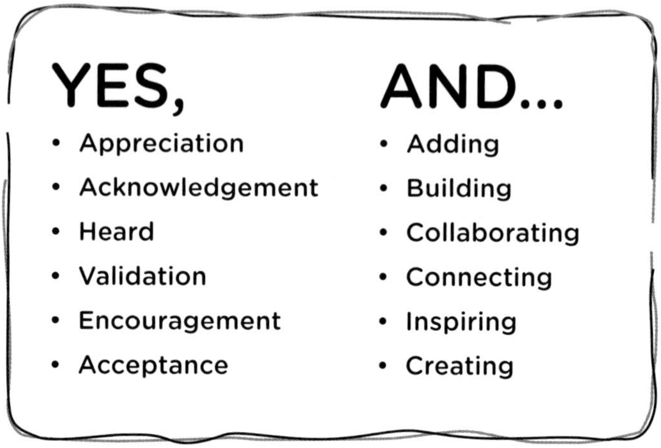

YES,

- Appreciation
- Acknowledgement
- Heard
- Validation
- Encouragement
- Acceptance

AND...

- Adding
- Building
- Collaborating
- Connecting
- Inspiring
- Creating

Figure 2.1 Encourage spontaneity with the Yes, And protocol[10]

The *Yes, And* protocol is just as powerful in business as it is on stage. Simply hearing the word *yes* is reassuring. It affirms that what the speaker said has been heard and encourages the speaker to continue. But when the *yes* is followed with the word *and*, it gives people the opportunity to explore a new possibility that they might not have considered if they were working alone. Imagine a scenario in an agile team where a software developer and a customer are working closely together to define a new requirement...

> Customer: *"The user needs to be able to change the marketing preferences within the account..."*

> Developer: *"Yes, and they also need to be able to update their email notifications, too..."*

The collaboration contains a *yes* confirmation *and* an additional offer to build on. As such, both the customer and developer learn about part of a requirement that might be missing or identify a simpler way for the developer to build this functionality. The conversation is a positive one, where both parties are working equally towards a mutually beneficial solution.

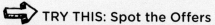 **TRY THIS: Spot the Offers**

During a technical discussion or retrospective, try to identify where offers are being made. Are some attendees making more offers than others? How are people responding to offers?

Blocks

Improv scenes, however, don't always rely solely on accepted offers (the *Yes, And* protocol). The opposite of an offer is a **block**. This can be anything an actor does to prevent action or progress. As an example, consider the coffee shop scene from the previous section. The first actor makes the same offer:

> *First Actor: "Good morning, sir..."*

But suppose the second actor responds with a block:

> *Second Actor: "Good morning. But I'm not here to buy coffee."*

Notice what has happened here. The second actor has said, "Yes, it is morning, *but* I'm not a customer." The scene is blocked by this negative response, the audience is concerned that their suggestion has been rejected, and the first actor must now work harder to create the next offer. That doesn't mean the second actor's response is necessarily a bad one (as I'll discuss later, blocks do have their purpose), but blocks are ineffective when used continually or habitually.

TRY THIS: Yes, But
During a technical discussion or retrospective, listen for blocking responses that start with "yes, but". How do they affect collaboration and dynamics in the room?

Blocking is a natural response when people feel threatened or unsafe. In an uncertain situation, people's instinct is to protect themselves rather than enable others. Blocking helps individuals maintain control, but it makes collaboration much more difficult.

I notice an excessive number of blocking responses in conversations within agile teams. This is perhaps not surprising given the uncertainty in software development, especially around customer requirements or technological strategy. Yet the habitual use of blocks can be damaging to creativity and teamwork.

On a recent coaching engagement, the Scrum team I was coaching had a particularly frosty relationship with their product owner. During my time, I could see the product owner was struggling with planning sessions, mainly due to how worn-down the development team had become from dealing with a complex, legacy system that was riddled with technical debt. I observed a great deal of negative energy in the planning sessions, especially when the development team was asked to take on new work. I helped to change this energy by simply changing the language and structure of how the team communicated with the product owner. I asked the team to apply the *yes, and* protocol using my 3D process (Duplicate, Describe, Develop):

Duplicate: Repeat back what the product owner has said.
            This step shows that you were actually listening. ("**Yes.**")

Describe: Find something within the suggestion that you like.
            Tell the product owner what it was and why you liked it.
            ("I agree with this part.")

Develop: Make a suggestion on how the idea could be improved,
            even if you think the idea is already good.
            ("**And,** here's an additional thought to consider.")

For example, going back to the team I coached that was struggling with technical debt, suppose the product owner had said, "I need you to redesign the registration page to make it quicker to sign up." A 3D response might be something like, "Yes. We could redesign the registration page as it's quite painful for users to fill in at the moment. And, it would be nice to clean up the defects in the password validation at the same time."

Several teams I have worked with who have used this 3D process have forged powerful and long-lasting customer relationships, and have gained a can-do reputation from those customers. **Creating an offer-rich environment should be a real area of focus for those in a leadership position of any agile team.**

 TRY THIS: Yes, And

Given an everyday conversation with one of your team members, make a purposeful attempt to start each of your responses as an offer, using the words **yes** and **and**. Note the behavioural and emotional changes each of you go through.

Selective Use of Blocks

Though offers are powerful tools, the selective use of blocks can sometimes be effective too, both in improvisational theatre and in business. To experienced improvisers, occasional blocks can jolt a story or situation into a different direction, provided the other actors or collaborators are equipped to deal with them. During a recent conversation, seasoned improviser and Comedy Store player Richard Vranch talked to me about the power of "getting your laugh on the block". He cautioned, though, that you need the support of other offers around you to pick the story back up again and continue to delight the audience.[11]

What Vranch was describing was an improviser's ability to transform a block into an offer, to inject life into a dying scene or story allowing it to continue forward.

To illustrate, I'll revisit the coffee shop example again...

First Actor: "*Good morning, sir...*" *(OFFER)*

Second Actor: "*Good morning. But I'm not here to buy coffee.*" *(BLOCK)*

First Actor: "*OK, OK, mister. I don't want any trouble. Just take the money, and* **please** *don't hurt me!*" *(OFFER)*

Notice that an entirely new storyline, about a coffee shop robbery, has unfolded in the recovering offer.

Similarly, when agile teams or individuals are faced with a blocking response, if they respond with a new offer, they can open the door to something new and unexpected.

People's ability to collaborate is measured by their ability to create and accept offers from any angle and their resistance to respond with blocks.

TRY THIS: Block into Offer
Can you think of a recent event where you (or someone in your team) have been handed a block and consequently turned it into an offer?

Remaining Open

In order to respond with a new offer, instead of a block, improv actors must remain open to change. While it is true that blocking is a natural response when faced with a loss of control or predictability, improvisers who resist change slow progress and can even bring a scene to a complete halt.

The same thing can happen in business. In software development, the word *change* is associated with additional cost. If requirements change, the cost of delivery increases and customers are unhappy. As I write this, I can almost hear the words "Yes, but" in my head. It's just so easy for people to block change, purely by resisting the uncertainty it brings.

Agile teams can be more spontaneous purely by accepting that change will indeed occur, and then, when it does, by asking how that change could have a positive impact. Accepting change in a software project gives customers what they really want, which *yes*, may require some re-work. *And* the benefit of that re-work could result in delivering customer value earlier, and maybe even finishing the project sooner than expected. Looking at change in a more positive way, as an *offer*, allows action to occur.

This reminds me of a recent camping holiday with my family. We were involved in an organised den-building challenge, where I, my wife, and my two children were tasked with building a den from old branches and leaves scattered around the forest. When we completed our challenge, we were asked to create some rules for living in our newly built woodland abode. One of the camp helpers walked over to give her input and said to my daughter Jocelyn:

"What shouldn't we do in your den?"

Jocelyn shrugged her shoulders and seemed confused by the negative phrasing, probably because it was challenging her creative and open attitude. In response, the camp helper asked a follow-up question to help elicit the desired response (we shouldn't light a match in our den):

"What would happen if your den caught fire?"

To Jocelyn, the answer to the question was now obvious. And it proved to me what being spontaneous is actually about. With a knowing smile, Jocelyn responded with:

"We could toast marshmallows on it!"

Creating Change

As shown in the discussion of offers and blocks, a spontaneous response doesn't *react* to change – it *creates* new change. In the quest for organisational agility, there are no blueprints to follow. Even the companies who have had success, such as Spotify, maintain that the journey is "still in progress".[12] Many people I meet are following an agile path because they need to be able to respond to change, as the agile manifesto suggests. What they might not yet understand, however, is that they will be best able to respond to that change as they grow more able to react spontaneously in the face of uncertainty. **Agile teams that can embrace their spontaneity will open up avenues that might have remained unexplored otherwise.**

In their quest for spontaneity, individuals must be aware that people *constantly* filter their imaginations. Because they fear being seen as insane, rude, or boring, individuals tend to reject their most obvious thoughts, which is why many people freeze when they are asked to be creative on the spot. Yet even when they are aware of the negative effect of subconscious filtering, people will continue to find it difficult to change these ingrained behaviours without the openness and collaboration of those around them.

The first step is to create a safe environment for the team (see Chapter 1, "Safety"). Then, take the initiative to relieve some of your teammates' creative burdens by making a conscious effort to create offers. Likewise, when presented with an offer, or even if you perceive a block, deliberately respond with an offer instead of a block. In the resulting offer-rich environment, spontaneous change will flourish and the team's true imaginations will begin to emerge.

Consider this chapter and indeed this whole book as my first offer to you. Specifically, I've included several spontaneity games in the next part of this chapter.

How will you choose to respond?

PLAY

SPONTANEITY

GAMES

Spontaneity Games

The games in this chapter aim to explain the use of offers and blocks to help teams collaborate more effectively.

I AM A TREE[13]

Players	Timebox	Energy Level	Individual	Team	Visual	Verbal	Physical	Scenario
5–7	15 mins	✳✳✳✳✳	✳✳	✳✳✳✳	✳✳✳	✳✳✳✳	✳✳✳✳	Team Building

Synopsis

A group of three players will build a scene using three offers. The initial offer is "I am a tree." The other players in the group will add to this offer with the aim of making the scene more interesting each time. Look for and commend good offers, those that open up more options. Also point out any blocks, describing how they narrow the other players' choices.

Script:

Walk the group members through an example using two volunteer players.

FACILITATOR: "One member of the group will start the scene by entering the circle and stating, 'I am a tree,' while also acting like a tree."

The facilitator does this, acting as the first player.

FACILITATOR: "The next player enters the scene by stating, 'I am…' and choosing an appropriate word and action to make the scene more interesting. For instance, the player might say, 'I am a bird,' and flap their arms like a bird."

Have a second volunteer player act this out.

FACILITATOR: "Now, we need a third person to complete this scene."

Instruct the second volunteer player to act this out, saying, 'I am a gardener,' and miming raking the ground.

FACILITATOR: "Now the scene is complete."

FACILITATOR: "Another scene will now follow. The first player who entered the scene (in this case the tree) will leave and choose one other player to remove from the scene as well."

For example, you could say, "I'll take away the bird." Then, you and the second player (the bird) should leave the scene.

FACILITATOR: "Now the gardener is the first element of the next scene. We always start a new scene with 'I am a…'"

The remaining player will start the new scene with the same character, saying, "I am a gardener." At this point, encourage other players to enter the scene so that the game can continue and new scenes can emerge. Anyone can jump in at any time, but as soon as the scene reaches three elements, it restarts.

Side Coaching

"How can we make this scene more interesting?"

"State the obvious. Don't think too much – go with your instinct."

Speculation

"What made the scenes more interesting?"

"What made the scenes less interesting?"

"What inspired you to contribute?"

Suggestions

Experiment with emotions rather than purely physical objects. Examples include "I am rage" or "I am tension".

COLLABORATIVE DRAWING[14]

Players	Timebox	Energy Level	Individual	Team	Visual	Verbal	Physical	Scenario
2–10	15 mins	*	***	***	****	*	*	Anytime

Synopsis

This game involves players creating a drawing on a single piece of paper, taking it in turns to hold the pen or pencil. The process helps address how collaborating with others involves accepting change and enabling creativity.

Script

Split into pairs. Each pair needs a plain piece of paper and one pen to share.

FACILITATOR: "You are going to create a picture between you, but you must only draw one line at a time. You can't discuss your drawing verbally. In order to start, one player will draw a pair of eyes in the middle of the page. That player will then pass the pen to the other player who will draw one line. The pen then passes back and forth this way, with each player drawing one line at a time, until the pair deem the drawing complete."

Starting with a pair of eyes gives the drawing an initial offer to work from. Give the pairs a chance to complete their drawings and enjoy the creativity that occurs.

FACILITATOR: "When your drawing is complete, you must give it a title. But this time you can only write one letter at a time."

Allow group members to share their drawings and enjoy their collaborative output.

Speculation

"Are you pleased with your drawing?"

"What made it a success? Or a failure?"

"Were there any moments of frustration or disappointment?"

"Did you filter any ideas instead of drawing them? Why?"

Suggestions

In a retrospective, repeat this game, albeit on a much larger scale, to set the scene, gather data, or summarise the output from the iteration.

In a planning session, use the same techniques to create whiteboard designs or wireframes.

ONE-WORD STAND-UP[15]

Players	Timebox	Energy Level	Individual	Team	Visual	Verbal	Physical	Scenario
5–9	15 mins	*	* * *	* * *	*	* * * *	*	Daily Stand-up

Synopsis

Players give their updates in pairs, but each person can use only one word at a time. This encourages the players to be more spontaneous and to have some fun during the stand-up meeting.

Script

FACILITATOR: "In today's stand-up, you will give your update as a pair but must switch speakers after each word. The normal three questions apply, but you will answer with what each of you did yesterday, what each of you will do today, and what is blocking either of you."

Allow each pair to give their updates in this manner, and expect some awkward silences and sniggers along the way.

Continue this until all the players have spoken and the team has synchronised the day's work.

Suggestions

Encourage other players to ask clarifying questions. The pair's responses still have to be given one word, per speaker, at a time.

Should any players be pairing during the iteration, try giving a combined update explaining what *we* did.

Experiment with larger group sizes, maybe three or four people.

WHAT'S IN THE BOX?[16]

Players	Timebox	Energy Level	Individual	Team	Visual	Verbal	Physical	Scenario
2–10	10 mins	***	****	**	**	*****	***	Anytime

Synopsis

Players pull items from an imaginary box that their partners are holding. This game allows players to exercise their spontaneity and to understand how important a partner can be in helping to unlock one's own creativity, purely by saying "yes".

Script

Players split into pairs for this exercise. The game is best explained by the facilitator walking through the exercise with a volunteer player.

FACILITATOR: "I am holding an imaginary box. My partner is going to mime pulling objects out of that box. Then, my partner must tell me what has been pulled out. Whatever my partner says, I must agree."

Demonstrate. For example:

Have a volunteer player hold the imaginary box. Mime pulling out a delicate object while keeping it at arm's length.

FACILITATOR: "It's a tarantula!"

At this point, the role of the box-carrier needs to be explained further…

FACILITATOR: "Now, the person holding the imaginary box must verify the object by saying 'Yes, of course it's a tarantula!' before that object can be put down."

Wait for the response…

VOLUNTEER: "Yes! Of course it's a tarantula!"

FACILITATOR: "And the game continues as more items are pulled out of the box and are accepted by the other player each time, like so."

Mime pulling out a very small object held between thumb and forefinger.

FACILITATOR: "It's a paper clip!"

VOLUNTEER: "Yes! Of course it's a paper clip!"

Allow the remainder of the players to break off into their pairs to try it for themselves.

Side Coaching

"Look down into the box. Is there something soft in there? Is there something from the kitchen?"

"Try not to filter your ideas. Say what you see…"

Shift

After five minutes, ask the players holding the imaginary boxes to hand them over to their partners and reverse the roles in the game.

Speculation

"Did you find the ideas came more quickly as the game went on?"

"What allowed your ideas to flow?"

"How did your partner help?"

"Did you screen any ideas before you said them? If so, why?"

Suggestions

Switch pairs and allow the players to repeat the game with someone else. Raise the subject of filtering ideas, and whether anyone relaxed those filters during the game.

Discuss how repeating old ideas isn't a bad thing – being creative isn't always about being original.

Try the same game but ask the person holding the box to name the objects this time as the other player mimes pulling them out. The person miming grabbing the objects must always agree to (and react to) the name. Does this change the dynamic?

DELIGHT[17]

Players	Timebox	Energy Level	Individual	Team	Visual	Verbal	Physical	Scenario
2–10	10 mins	***	****	**	**	*****	**	Anytime

Synopsis

Players split into pairs and tell a short story, but one of them can only add to the story by using the word "No". This game helps the players deal with blocks by countering with alternative offers to allow the story to continue, and shows how continuous blocking can prevent action.

Script

Allow the players to split into pairs. This game is best demonstrated with a volunteer player to explain how the game works.

FACILITATOR: "Marie and I are going to tell a story together. However, Marie, you can only say the word 'No' to help tell the story. Do you understand?"

(The volunteer player at this point may say "No" purely for comedic effect!)

FACILITATOR: "OK. Here we go."

The facilitator starts to tell a first-person story that also involves the volunteer. For example:

FACILITATOR: "I can remember one afternoon when Marie and I went out for a walk in the forest. The sun was shining…"

VOLUNTEER: "No".

At this point the facilitator (as the lead player) has been blocked by the volunteer player and must quickly suggest an alternative offer with the aim of "delighting" the volunteer. If the volunteer doesn't like the alternative, that player can reject it again, until an acceptable response is mentioned.

FACILITATOR: "It was pouring with rain…"

VOLUNTEER: "No".

FACILITATOR: "It was snowing…"

No response from the volunteer indicates that you have found an acceptable counter offer. And the story can continue…

Once the basic process has been observed, encourage the other players to try telling a new story in this way as a pair.

Side Coaching

"Look around you for inspiration!"

"Watch your partner's reactions; you should try and delight them!"

Shift

After five minutes, stop the groups and ask them to switch roles with the other player.

Speculation

"How did you deal with hearing the word 'No' continuously?"

"Did the story ever grind to a complete halt?"

"What allowed the story to continue?"

"Were you both pleased with the outcome?"

"How does this relate to how we work with our customers?"

Suggestions

Play the game again with different partners.

Encourage both players to act/mime the story as they tell it, which shows acceptance and openness from both players.

Try a variation by adding the question "what happens next?" which can be used to switch the storyteller after the word "No" has been used. This encourages the "No" player to suggest the alternative and carry the story on.

STORYTELLING

There was an explosion in an old cottage because there was a magic wand that belonged to a magician. He magicked a potion. To make the potion, the magician used poison, so when the baddies come to eat him, he can throw it onto them. The magician would sneakily go into the kitchen and they would drink it. Behind the mirror in the kitchen is where the magician kept the poison. The last one. "I hope this works!" he said. Inside another jar there was a storm. There was another enormous jar behind the mirror in the kitchen, which contained a dragon. The magician opened the jar, and chopped the dragon's head off. It wasn't a real dragon and he put it in the pot with the potion. The magician was wearing a mask because if he put the poison in without the mask, he would die.

Jocelyn Goddard (age 5)

STORYTELLING

The joy that both of my young children get when I read them a story never diminishes. Equally, they are my harshest critics when my storytelling doesn't provide enough realism. "Do the voices too, Daddy!" they cry.

People's love for stories doesn't lessen as they get older. A great story on screen or stage can hold my attention for hours. A story is not simply a sequence of events, as one definition in Merriam-Webster would suggest.[1] Instead, I define a "good story" as one that stimulates intrigue and holds my attention.

But what does all this have to do with software development? I believe that agile teams become more engaged when they harness the enjoyment and escapism that storytelling provides – when they re-imagine their projects as stories in their own right. Stories have been part of human evolution since the first cave paintings were discovered thousands of years ago, and still remain as a fundamental method of communicating.

The previous chapters have explored how a safe environment and increasing spontaneity are powerful tools for improvisation theatre. Yet without a good grasp of how to tell stories, actors can be safe and spontaneous but remain dull and uninteresting as performers.

In this chapter, I will explain the simple principles that improv actors use to help them build engaging and interesting stories on the fly, as they have no book or screenplay to fall back on.

For each of the principles, I will give some examples of how I have applied them in scenarios with the agile teams I have worked with over the years. Well, if you are sitting comfortably, then I will begin…

Importance of Storytelling

In his blog post, "The Science of Storytelling", Leo Widrich, co-founder and COO of Buffer, suggests that the human brain becomes more active when people tell or listen to stories.[2] If you were to read a PowerPoint presentation that contains only bullet points, only the language-decoding parts of your brain would be stimulated. However, should the presenter tell you a story, not only are the language-decoding parts of your brain activated, but any other area of your brain that you would use when experiencing the events of the story is also stimulated.

This theory was tested in 2006 when researchers in Spain ran a series of experiments where a number of participants were asked to read words with strong odour associations, along with neutral words, while their brains were scanned by a functional magnetic resonance imaging (fMRI) machine. When the participants read words such as coffee or perfume, their primary olfactory cortex lit up. Yet when they read words such as chair and key, this area remained dark. Similar research from the Laboratory of Language Dynamics in France found that words describing motion also stimulate regions of the brain distinct from the language-processing areas. Phrases such as "He kicked the ball" trigger responses from the motor cortex, the part of the brain that coordinates body movement, even down to the specific region or cortex that controls leg movement.[3]

In simple terms, when people hear a story unfold they develop empathy. They feel the physical and emotional ups and downs that the storyteller describes.

In improvisational theatre, the role of the actors on stage is to hold the attention of every audience member from the start of the performance until the end. Because the actors have no script or director to look to for external guidance, they have to rely on their own ability to create compelling stories and tell them in an engaging way. To do this effectively, they use the following key elements of storytelling:

- keeping it simple;
- reincorporating the past;
- relating to the characters; and
- finishing the story.

Keeping it Simple

A good story is a simple one. You can distil most iconic movies down to a basic premise or what Hollywood screenwriters call a hook.[4] See if you can guess the names of the movies from the following hooks:

1. There's a bomb on a crowded city bus. If the bus slows below 50 miles an hour, the bomb will go off.
2. A massive great white shark terrorises a beach resort, and the local sheriff must find a way to stop it.
3. An FBI agent seeks the counsel of a convicted psychopath to help track down a serial killer.
4. A Roman general is betrayed by the emperor's son, and he returns to Rome as a gladiator to seek his revenge.[1]

Many improv troupes will interact with the audience in order to create an initial theme for their story. The London-based improv troupe The Comedy Store Players, for example, will ask for a well-known fictional character and an unrelated household object to create story titles, such as:

- Harry Potter and the Toaster;
- Sherlock Holmes and the MP3 Player; and
- Bruce Banner and the Cheese Grater.

The simplicity of these titles leaves more to the imagination of both the improvisers and the audience, and allows a story to emerge. This gives the improvisers more options to create a plot that is not just interesting to the audience, but also to the performers. And as the story unfolds, the simple system of offers and blocks gives the actors the bandwidth to exercise their creativity. (See Chapter 2, "Spontaneity", for more on offers and blocks.)

Using one of the titles, The Comedy Store Players then play a game called Die. In this game, all of the performers are on the stage. One of the performers begins telling a story based on the chosen title. Then, when an offstage director points directly at another performer, that performer must pick up the story thread and continue the story. The tricky part is that the director can decide to change which storyteller s/he is pointing

---

[1] Answers: 1) *Speed,* 2) *Jaws,* 3) *Silence of the Lambs,* 4) *Gladiator.*

at, at any point in time. Should an improviser pause, hesitate, or crumble into incoherency, the members of the audience will shout "DIE!!" Then, that improviser is out of the game. The simple story title lets the players explore how the lead character came into contact with such a household object, as that is what the audience wants to know. (For more on The Comedy Store Players and what agile teams can learn from them, see Afterword, "The Comedy Store Players".)

Simple hooks or titles can be useful to an agile team, especially if the team is using user stories. User stories are a worthy addition to any agile process. They originated in the eXtreme Programming community but are now widely used by many agile teams. The standard definition of a user story is one that should fit on a small index card in the form, "As a user, I want a feature so that I get some benefit." The acceptance criteria are written on the back of the same card. **My concern is that the word "story" has become superfluous, as these artefacts have become a means to capture technical information as documentation rather than making a connection between the character and the reader.**

The title of a user story should create intrigue and options. "Add password encryption to database" is prescriptive and leaves little to the imagination of anyone involved in implementing it. However, the title "Improve password security" contains unknowns that will need clarification and discussion. Strangely, many of the agile teams I work with seem to have forgotten that user stories were designed as a promise for a conversation rather than a replacement for a conversation. An intriguing title can help stimulate that initial conversation between the requestor and the implementer.

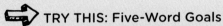 **TRY THIS: Five-Word Goals**
In an agile planning session, ask the team members to
simplify their commitment into a series of five-word
statements, such as "A user can update preferences"
or "Rebuild and refactor postroom functionality".

Improvisation guru Keith Johnstone tells his students to "be obvious".[5]
Do what the audience expects and they will be delighted. For example, in
the fictional title "Bruce Banner and the Cheese Grater", the audience is
expecting the cheese grater, in some way, to cause Bruce to become the
Hulk. Maybe he cuts his finger on it while making a sandwich? Maybe
he gets angry when his cheese hasn't been grated the right way? If the
actors try to avoid the simple flow of the story by trying to be too clever or
original, they risk confusing both audience and their fellow players alike –
ending up with a story that no one can follow or remember.

This strikes an immediate chord with one of the principles of the agile
manifesto, which stresses how simplicity, the art of maximising the
amount of work not done, is essential to agile teams.[6] Yet simplicity does
not come naturally to us. As Steve Jobs once said, "Simple can be harder
than complex".[7]

The best example I see of this happens when I run The Ball Point Game,
a well-known agile game initially devised by Boris Gloger, and a great, fun
way for new agile teams to learn the benefits of an agile approach. The
aim of the game is to iteratively create a system that can transport small
balls among the players while adhering to a few simple rules:

- Each ball must touch each player at least once as it moves through
  the system.
- Each ball must have "air-time" between each player.
- A ball cannot be passed to adjacent players.
- Each ball must return back to its original starting point.

For every ball that passes through the team's system and follows these rules, the team scores a point. By playing the game in small iterations, the team is encouraged to improve their system (and consequently the number of points) each time.

I won't risk the wrath of other agile trainers by giving away solutions here. In essence, though, teams increase the flow of balls by simplifying the process and eliminating waste.[8] For me, the beauty of the game is that there are many system designs that will work and produce good results – and teams who experiment find those solutions more quickly.

However, in my experience, some players spend far too long analysing the mathematical algorithms to find the optimal (and usually the most complex) configuration to implement, at the risk of alienating those in the group who don't understand it. **And then, it seems, when we find a system that works well, the desire is to continue to add complexity to it rather than to simplify it.**

In the same way, agile teams today have many processes, frameworks, and methods at their disposal. What started out quite simple has now become complex. The combinations and permutations seem to be growing at pace. As I write, teams can choose from using Scrum and XP, Kanban and XP, ScrumBan, LeSS, and SAFe – and no doubt others will emerge. The list of tools designed to support these methods is even longer – and tools add an extra layer of complexity that clouds the process even further. **My default approach is always to start simple and resist the urge to add too much complexity too soon.**

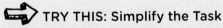 **TRY THIS: Simplify the Task**
Can you think of a complex scenario (in or out of the work context) where simplifying the solution has brought the same or better results?

Reincorporating the Past

Another simple principle that improvisers follow is **reincorporation**. To best explain this, I will attempt to make up a story as I write. In order to start my story, I consulted with my Chief Creativity Officer, Miss Jocelyn Goddard, for a subject for my story. Unsurprisingly she chose princesses, her specialist subject. My story attempts and subsequent conversations with Jocelyn are shown below.

So here goes.

A princess rides through the forest on horseback. She stops riding to pick some flowers. The princess walks towards a beautiful waterfall. She sees a frog sitting on a rock, but the frog jumps away. She follows the frog to a hole in the riverbank. She crawls through a tunnel until she finds a large staircase. On the staircase, there is a small boy crying.

I stop because I am wandering aimlessly. When I read aloud what I've written so far to Jocelyn, she frowns and asks, "Why did the frog run away? Why is the boy crying?" To help answer these questions and to provide some cohesion, I need to write a new version of this story that reintroduces previous elements of the story. I start again.

A princess rides through the forest on horseback. She stops riding to pick some flowers. The flowers lead the princess towards a beautiful waterfall. Underneath the waterfall is a frog sitting on a rock. The frog sniffs the princess's flowers and with a huge "A-choo!" he jumps away. The princess follows the frog to a hole in the riverbank. She crawls through a tunnel, which ends in a large staircase. On the staircase, there is a small boy crying. "I've lost my pet frog," he says.

I run this second iteration past Jocelyn, and the review is more positive. By connecting the frog to the waterfall, the flowers, and the boy, I've created a more compelling story. As a result, Jocelyn is more engaged and wants to know what happens next!

When improvisers tell unscripted stories they are always looking for ways to reintroduce anything the audience has seen or heard previously. **Being** creative or inventive can be as easy as reincorporating previous offers. Children have an uncanny instinct for this, as you will notice if you go back and re-read the story that Jocelyn imagined for me at the start of this chapter.

As an agile coach, I am constantly looking to help teams or individuals find their own solutions. When I find myself in a coaching conversation with individuals, I try to help them tell their own stories and make the narrative connections that will move their stories – and situations – forward. Here are some examples of questions I've asked in recent coaching conversations (names have been changed for privacy) that have helped people make connections:

- You mentioned that Jenny was in the room. How did she react to your suggestion?
- Can you recall any other instances of that happening? How did you handle that before?
- When was the last time you felt like this?

What has happened in the past can be extremely useful to someone's development. Quite often, the source of what to do next can be found by making connections with events that have occurred previously. A regular retrospective is an obvious opportunity to help an agile team to start connecting previous events. But while many teams will spend time recalling previous events that occurred over the past few weeks, telling the story of the sprint or iteration could be a more powerful exercise.

TRY THIS: Connecting Photographs
Take photos of various events or images as they occur during the iteration. Aim for around 10 to 15 pictures. Attempt to reconnect the pictures in a storyboard format during the retrospective, and look for connections between them.

I feel retrospectives themselves can suffer if they focus too much on the things that blocked the team. As I stated in Chapter 2, "Spontaneity", continuous blocking prevents progress and stifles creative suggestion. A balanced retrospective should allow a team to build on positives and continue doing things that went well. **"What was the team doing well that they should do again?"** is a great question to encourage the team members to acknowledge any previous ideas or actions, and then incorporate them into this next chapter of their story.

Relating to the Characters

Back in 2012, story artist Emma Coats blogged about a series of narrative rules in use while she was working at Pixar, a company famed for its learning culture and for leading the way in animated movie-making in Hollywood. The first of these principles stated:

"You admire a character for trying more than their successes."[9]

An audience admires movie characters such as Indiana Jones, John McClane (*Die Hard*), and Ripley (*Alien*) for going beyond their own boundaries. The characters seem more realistic and human to us when we can empathise with their pain and struggles. **When the audience can relate to the character, the changes the character goes through become even more interesting to us.** The same can be true of anti-hero stories too, as a villain usually has to sacrifice something in order to become a hero: Gru from the animated movie *Despicable Me* is a good example of this.

This type of character development can be useful to an agile team too if we consider that the customers and users are characters in our own product development story. By identifying more with these characters, a development team can become much more in tune with customer requirements, and more sympathetic to the users' needs and issues.

A good user story, for example, should describe a change from the character's perspective. Well-written user stories are a great way to start to build empathy between these two parties.

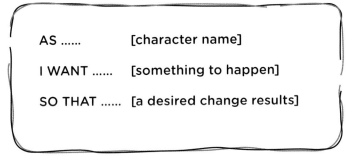

AS ......   [character name]

I WANT ......   [something to happen]

SO THAT ...... [a desired change results]

Figure 3.1 A user story template from a character's perspective

However, a user story will be even more engaging if the intended audience can relate to both the character and the problem or situation they are experiencing. Many user stories I see jump straight into the solution before defining and understanding what the problem really is. To counter this, I coach the use of an iterative process when writing a user story, which starts with the *who* and the *why* of the story first of all. I'll attempt to illustrate with a user story from my daughter Jocelyn.

First Iteration:

> **AS Jocelyn I WANT [something]**
>
> **SO THAT I can get to sleep**

By substituting in the word "something", we focus firstly on the who and the why of the story. In this case, the *who* is Jocelyn, and the *why* is that she wants to get to sleep. Some teams will have detailed personas that help team members identify with their users or customers,[10] but luckily for me as Jocelyn's father, I have already experimented with several options, so I can help her find some appropriate solutions. I may then present back several different choices for Jocelyn to think about.

Second Iteration:

> **AS Jocelyn I WANT a cup of hot milk**
>
> **SO THAT I can get to sleep**

> **AS Jocelyn I WANT my soft bunny**
>
> **SO THAT I can get to sleep**

> **AS Jocelyn I WANT a hug**
>
> **SO THAT I can get to sleep**

In my case, I know that Jocelyn will probably want all three of these solutions. A customer or product owner, however, will likely value some options more than others. The members of an agile team can even provide estimates of the effort involved for each alternative to help the product owner or customer make a more informed choice. Once all parties have made the connections between the character, the problem, and the potential solutions, and chosen one solution for implementation, they can agree on the finer details in the form of acceptance criteria for the story.

> **ACCEPTANCE CRITERIA:**
> - **Served in pink cup**
> - **Half full**
> - **Served no hotter than 50°C**

A team that follows this iterative formula will benefit from a deeper understanding of the problem itself, and will feel that they have been part of the story creation and development. Do not underestimate how powerful these connections can be if fostered effectively.

Finishing the Story

Once an audience has established a connection with the principal characters in a story, related to their struggles, and seen an emotional or physical change occur in them, the audience will want closure. They want to tie up loose ends and leave the auditorium feeling satisfied. This conclusion is so vital that Coats' Pixar rules of storytelling state, "Come up with your ending before you figure out your middle".[11]

But ending a story can be hard, especially for improvisers on stage who don't use a pre-written, tested script or have the chance to stop mid-performance to discuss how the plot will be resolved. As such, improvisers rely on resolving character or event connections in order to give the actors and audience the closure they desire.

Software development teams gain the same satisfaction from reaching the end of a work package or from seeing a number of software tests pass as a new feature is developed. Once again, user stories can help a team achieve this by specifying the acceptance criteria of the story. If I were bringing Jocelyn a cup of hot milk, I would ensure that I checked her acceptance criteria before I started making it and again before I delivered it, because otherwise it could be a lengthy process!

> **AS Jocelyn I WANT a cup of hot milk**
>
> **SO THAT I can get to sleep**

> **ACCEPTANCE CRITERIA:**
> - **Served in pink cup**
> - **Half full**
> - **Served no hotter than 50°C**

One of the many benefits of working in iterations is that a team reaches closure on their work every two or three weeks. This is a chance for the team to take a breath, look back, and take some pride in what they have achieved. Teams that continually leave work incomplete or half-finished, extend their timeboxes, or simply roll on to the next iteration without stopping are missing out on the motivational side effects that ending the story offers.

 TRY THIS: Find a Finish

Finishing a story is tough. Ask the team members to tell a complete story in two minutes, using only one word at a time, each. Observe whether they manage to bring the story to a satisfying conclusion when the time expires.

Making Connections through Stories

Telling a story develops empathy between the audience and the story's characters. A good storyteller is good at creating empathy. When we relate to the characters more closely, their problems can become our problems, allowing us to understand our customers and collaborate more closely with them. However, it's no use being good at storytelling if there is no story to tell.

In agile development, a good story is what galvanises the team members together during an iteration or project. Agile software development should embrace emergence in design and build, as much as improvisers embrace telling a story without a pre-defined script. Aim for a simple storyline so that development teams have more bandwidth to explore their creative options before deciding how to solve their problem. Remember, too, that being creative is not always about original thought; team members can reincorporate previous offers or solutions to help them connect the dots. Finally, don't forget to finish. Team members will gain more momentum when they see a particular story or chapter end before they move on.

Well-written user stories can be the chapters within the overall story of a project. If the story is interesting enough, and it's being told in an engaging way, you may discover an agile team that can motivate itself to keep turning the pages of the book.

What story is your team telling?

PLAY
STORYTELLING
GAMES

Storytelling Games

The games in this chapter are aimed at how to create stories, develop characters through change, and keep the audience interested.

SWEDISH STORY[12]

Players	Timebox	Energy Level	Individual	Team	Visual	Verbal	Physical	Scenario
5–7	5 mins	*	*****	**	*	****	*	Retro-spective

Synopsis

One player tells a story, absorbing suggested offers from the other players. The player must attempt to reconnect the offers back into the story and come to some conclusion within the timebox. This game encourages the player to cope with the emergent nature of the story being told, especially as the player lacks explicit control over the content.

Script

Illustrate the game by acting as the first player.

FACILITATOR: "In order to start the story, we need the lead character's first name and a physical location to give the story some context."

FACILITATOR: "OK. Once we have that information, the storytelling player can begin. To give you an example, I'll tell the first story. When I reach a point in the story where other players can influence a change, I will point to you for a cue."

Begin the story.

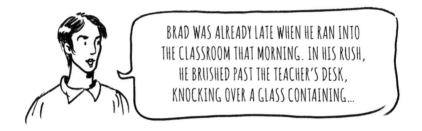

Point to other players and wait for a suggestion.

Using the new offer, continue the story.

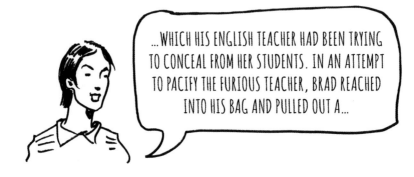

Point again.

And so on…

Expect the other players to block the action, purely for laughs, but try to reconnect previous parts of the story to encourage better offers from the audience.

Speculation

"What made the story interesting?"

"How engaged did you feel?"

"What increased/decreased your engagement?"

"What is a good story? If so, what made it good?"

Suggestions

In a retrospective, ask one of the team members to tell the story of the iteration or sprint, allowing the other players to throw in words when a break or pause occurs.

Try the same technique in a daily stand-up setting, giving updates as short stories.

WORD-AT-A-TIME STORYTELLING[13]

Players	Timebox	Energy Level	Individual	Team	Visual	Verbal	Physical	Scenario
4–10	5 mins	*	**	****	*	****	*	Anytime

Synopsis

This classic improv game is simple enough to explain, but harder to play. The players must learn to let go of their own plotlines and let the story truly emerge. It's also a good vehicle to coach how to make stories more compelling.

Script

Gather the players in a circle.

FACILITATOR: "We are going to tell a story one word at a time, passing the story around the circle as we go. When you say a word, you point to the person who's going to say the next word in the story. You don't need to say the punctuation marks. When you reach the end of a sentence, just start the next sentence, as you would in normal speech."

It may help some groups to give them the first line of the story to help them start, such as "once upon a time" or "one day long ago".

Side Coaching

"Make eye contact! Inspire each other!"

Should the story break down, encourage the group to throw their arms in the air and shout "AGAIN!" This makes failure acceptable and allows the group to try again.

Speculation

"Who created the story?"

"What made it more interesting?"

"Which words were the offers?"

"Which words were the blocks?"

Suggestions

Try the game again, but ask the group to give the story a title (still one word at a time) before the story begins. How does this change the story flow?

Highlight the blocks you heard in the game. Stalling progress by adding an adjective (the big, hairy, ugly, smelly...) is a form of blocking in itself.

Give the group a story structure before you begin to help them shape the story. This can be as simple as, "Go somewhere, find something bad, and then escape from it." This helps define a beginning, middle, and an end to the story.

GOLDFISH BOWL[14]

Players	Timebox	Energy Level	Individual	Team	Visual	Verbal	Physical	Scenario
5–10	10 mins	***	*****	****	**	****	**	Retrospective

Synopsis

A group of players writes down suggestions or quotes on slips of paper and puts them into a large container (typically the goldfish bowl from which the game gets its name). Two players then tell a story and, at various points, take suggestions from the bowl, to which they have to adapt.

When played in a retrospective, players can tell their own stories about the iteration that has just occurred, and also include some written offers from their fellow players.

Script

The group members will need access to several slips of paper and pens to write down their suggestions. You can use a bowl, an empty waste paper basket, a shoebox, or whatever you have to hand to hold the slips of paper.

FACILITATOR: "Write down any events that occurred during the iteration – try to use no more than five words. Write each one on a slip of paper and put it into the bowl/basket/box."

Ask for two volunteers to play out a scene in which they are informally discussing the iteration between themselves, while the other players observe the scene.

FACILITATOR: "When you feel the story is approaching an event that occurred, reach into the bowl/basket/box and read out that suggestion. Try to include characters and tell a story to the audience."

Allow the volunteer players to discard any duplicate events they pull out. Play in short rounds, and rotate the players around if you still have lots of paper slips left.

Speculation

"What emotions did we see during the conversation?"

"Did any positive suggestions emerge?"

"Which events had the biggest impact on the story?"

Suggestions

Instead of using events, ask for quotes from the team, perhaps their own thoughts or something they overheard from elsewhere during the iteration.

Experiment with multiple containers, each one holding a different type of suggestion: events, quotes, emotions, adjectives, and so on.

Try varying the game by adding more players at various points to add depth to the storytelling and keep the other team members interested.

LINK THE ITEMS[15]

Players	Timebox	Energy Level	Individual	Team	Visual	Verbal	Physical	Scenario
5–7	10 mins	✻	✻✻✻✻✻	✻✻✻	✻	✻✻✻✻	✻	Anytime

Synopsis

The players must attempt to link seemingly unrelated words into a short story or fable. This process helps the players practise making connections between offers, which helps develop their storytelling ability.

Script

Form a circle of players.

FACILITATOR: "Each of us is going to tell a short story. When it's your turn to tell a story, you will ask for three unrelated words from the rest of the group. You then have to somehow incorporate the words into your story. Story plot and length are entirely up to you."

Give the players a little time to prepare and to repeat the suggestions over in their heads a few times before they start telling their stories.

Speculation

"Did anyone decide on the full extent of their story before they started telling it?"

"Did anyone connect two items together in the hope the third would reveal itself?"

"Which stories did the other players enjoy the most?"

Suggestions

The practice of naming unrelated, random words is a good game within itself, particularly to practise spontaneity. Challenge players to try to list as many random words as they can without repetition or association. Allow observing players to referee the game.

STORY SPINES[16]

Players	Timebox	Energy Level	Individual	Team	Visual	Verbal	Physical	Scenario
5–7	5 mins	*	****	***	***	****	***	Anytime

Synopsis

This improv game provides a model for players to understand the structure of a good story. It has many applications in an agile context, from planning games to retrospectives to user story writing.

Script

The basic structure of a story spine[17] is shown in the following table:

The Story Spine	Structure	Function
Once upon a time…	Beginning	The context of the story is given and the main character's routine is established
Every day…		
But, one day…	The Event	The main character breaks that routine
Because of that…	Middle	The consequences for breaking the routine
Because of that…		
Because of that…		
Until finally…	The Climax	The main character embarks on success or failure
And, ever since then…	End	The main character succeeds or fails, and a new routine is established

I would advise you write this down on a flipchart for players to refer to during the game.

FACILITATOR: "We are going to describe the spine of a story, passing the story around the circle as we go. When it's your turn, start your sentence with the next part of the story spine, then point to the person you want to carry on the next part."

Side Coaching

Ask "Does this story make sense?" when you sense the story is unclear. Give the players the chance to stop and restart if they are unhappy with the structure.

Speculation

"Can you break down the main character's journey?"

"Does the story come to a definitive end?"

"How do we know it's finished?"

"Have the right connections been made?"

Suggestions

In a retrospective, ask players to describe the story of the iteration they just experienced.

In a planning session, set a goal for the iteration using this template.

Break down user stories by discussing and agreeing upon the beginning and ending of the story spine. Then work out the tasks to achieve that, which stem from the middle of the story spine.

Pick some movies familiar to the team and try to write the story spines to describe the plot; ask other players to guess the title from the spine.

STATUS

Two actors are called on to the stage.
"Our actors need a place to set their scene, please…"
"A zoo!" calls someone from the audience. The scene begins.

The first actor strides purposefully across the stage, hands on hips,
clearly looking for someone. He calls, "Simmons? Where are you?"

The second actor, assuming the role of Simmons, immediately steps
up from behind the first actor and replies, "What's up, Boss?"

The audience can instantly identify the characters and their
relationship to each other, purely from the verbal and non-verbal
language the actors are using.

STATUS

Have you ever walked down the pavement and had an embarrassing "dance-off" with an oncoming pedestrian, where neither party can decide which side to walk on? If you have, then you have experienced what improvisers refer to as *status*.[1]

Merriam-Webster defines status as "the position or rank of someone or something when compared to others in a society, organization, group, etc".[2] I believe that all of us have a default status response. Going back to the pavement scenario, if your natural response when approached by an oncoming pedestrian is to step out of the way (and thereby into the road and danger), then you may find you often prefer a low-status position. Conversely, if your instinctive response would be to hug the wall furthest away from the traffic and refuse to give way, you may tend to prefer high-status responses.

Improv actors are taught to exploit these natural tendencies. Keith Johnstone tells his students, "You don't have to have a 'good idea' – just an 'alter-the-relationship'".[3] In other words, deliberately exaggerating status or changing status with the other players on stage is the very thing that makes a scene interesting.

The same is true for the collaboration that should occur in an agile environment – creativity in teams comes from the exchange and manipulation of ideas, which can be greatly enhanced by deliberate changes in status.

This chapter looks closely at how people identify status and how improvisers play with status to make change occur. An agile team can benefit from understanding status and can use this knowledge to increase their collaborative behaviour and flow of creative suggestions.

Recognising Status

Some of the most captivating double acts I remember from the screen have used status to perfection: Laurel and Hardy, Morecambe and Wise, Peter Cook and Dudley Moore, and Tom and Jerry to name a few. These duos tend to have one primarily high-status member and one primarily low-status member. Consider Figure 4.1, which portrays the two actors from the scene at the start of this chapter.

Figure 4.1 Simmons and "The Boss"

"The Boss" is the prototypical high-status character, someone who purports to have superior intelligence, stature, rank, experience, age, or wisdom. This actor demonstrates all of these in this depiction, from his larger size to his expression of haughty disdain. By comparison, "Simmons" is assuming a low-status position, deliberately making himself smaller and clasping his hands. He even appears to be cowering behind his higher-status employer. Note that **behavioural status is not necessarily the same as social status. On stage, you can play a low-status millionaire or a high-status tramp.**

What if you were to take a snapshot of your own team? What would you observe? The human brain is pre-programmed to identify even the most subtle status signals. A high-status team member may subconsciously stand with feet turned out and pause before answering questions. Alternatively, a low-status team member may fidget or stand with feet turned in when giving an update to the other team members.

At a recent workshop in London, Keith Johnstone explained how people notice signals as acute as blink rate – a high blink rate is associated with low status and vice versa. Individuals tend to hold eye contact when they are trying to take the high-status position; they tend to break that eye contact when they submit to a lower status. Army drill sergeants will never break eye contact with recruits while barking their orders, and the recruits will never look back into the eyes of their sergeants for fear of breaking rank. (I also advise you never to eyeball a male silverback gorilla at the zoo!)

Johnstone also said that another important signal people give is the distance between their heads and their hands. Touching your mouth as you look at someone is often perceived by the observer as a signal of low status while high-status players tend to fill the room or space as much as they can.

Low-Status Signals	High-Status Signals
High blink rate	Low blink rate
Head moves while speaking	Head still while speaking
Feet turned in	Feet turned out
Answer question immediately	Pause before answering questions
Break eye contact	Hold eye contact
Touch face and mouth	Touch others
Expose top teeth (bite lower lip)	Expose bottom teeth

Figure 4.2 High- and low-status signals[4]

Such acute non-verbal changes to postures and mannerisms were found to have a direct effect on the hormone changes people experience when they adopt them. In a psychological study by Carney, Cuddy and Yap in 2010, 42 participants (26 females and 16 males) were randomly assigned high- and low-status poses. They were asked to hold those positions for one minute each. From analysing the saliva samples gathered from the participants, the results showed that the high-status body language poses caused an increase in the dominance hormone testosterone and a reduction in the stress hormone cortisol. Conversely, low-status postures resulted in a decrease in testosterone in the participants and an increase in cortisol. The study proves how people's posture and movements affect their behaviour, both physiologically and psychologically, and also how that behaviour could affect the responses of others around them.[5]

 TRY THIS: Identifying Status
Take five minutes each day to stop work and watch the status behaviours and exchanges in your team. Keep the results to yourself. Observing status will help you gain an understanding of the subtle status signals that occur each day.

Power of the Status Switch

Once you can observe what status signals people give off, the next step is to understand how small changes in status affect outcomes. Consider, for example, the depiction of Simmons and his employer in Figure 4.3. Simmons is smiling and looking superior after "The Boss" steps in the elephant dung that Simmons has failed to remove from the floor (purposefully or not!). Notice, too, how their relationship develops when this kind of natural status switch occurs. These status switches are where the audience becomes absorbed into the scene. As the actors change, the story becomes more interesting to watch.

Figure 4.3 A simple status switch between Simmons and "The Boss"

Playing with status can affect agile projects in a similar way. For example, when I was working as a ScrumMaster on one of my first agile projects at BT (British Telecom), I had the following conversation with the product owner of the project.

Product owner: I need these extra features to be included in this sprint. One of our major customers is depending on it.

ScrumMaster (me): Of course, I understand. We'll see what we can do…

For those of you unfamiliar with Scrum terminology, the ScrumMaster's primary job is to protect the team and the process. The product owner's role is to ensure that the right product gets built on time and on budget. Some tension naturally exists between these two roles and goals – to provide balance. In this instance, the product owner made a high-status demand and I chose an easy, non-confrontational, low-status response. With hindsight, I would have played this conversation differently.

To demonstrate why that is, I am going to replay that scenario, this time changing my response, to see if I might have achieved a more advantageous outcome. Note the offers and blocks that are a natural part of this conversation. (Offers are covered in detail in Chapter 2, "Spontaneity". Briefly, offers are positive suggestions intended to move a situation forward, as opposed to blocks, which require both parties to move in an alternative direction.)

Product owner: I need these extra features to be included in this sprint. One of our major customers is depending on it. [Offer]

ScrumMaster (me): That's a risk. We stand to reduce the quality of the features in progress if we accept a change right now. [Block]

Notice that this time I match the product owner's status by exhibiting knowledge and experience and by providing evidence that the product owner might not be aware of. At this point, the product owner and I are at a stalemate. To make some progress, someone's status needs to change ever so slightly.

For example, the product owner might respond with a lower-status response, acknowledging the block and making an alternative offer.

Product owner: Good point. When is a better time to bring this to the team's attention? [Alternative offer]

ScrumMaster (me): We have a product backlog refinement session tomorrow morning. That will give you an idea of the effort required by the team. You should be able to set expectations with the client from there.

These kinds of subtle status challenges are almost certainly occurring within your own team, even now. Other examples might be a low-status junior tester presenting a high-status senior developer with a defect found in the code or conversely a high-status senior tester challenging a low-status junior tester regarding the thoroughness of a test plan.

Where there is a gulf in status, or a refusal to change status, progress will be slow and awkward. While status *extremes* are entertaining on stage (and indeed easier for improvisers to perform), *subtle* status changes allow the two actors on stage to really connect and to appear much more interesting to the audience, as this is where a more natural collaboration can occur.

The same is true in business. Even though status is far less obvious than it is portrayed on stage, individuals still can take small steps to encourage status changes within their own team. For example, asking a team member who exhibits lower-status behaviours to take ownership of a meeting or oversee a process not only boosts that person's confidence, but also increases status among peers. Similarly, asking junior members of the team to speak first during planning sessions or retrospectives adjusts their status in relation to the more senior members of the team. Both of these subtle actions can help make lower-status team members feel more comfortable when expressing new ideas or exposing hidden problems. **Identifying those subtle changes in status can be the first step in learning how to collaborate within an agile team.**

➪ TRY THIS: The Status Chair
Place a chair in the middle of the room, and try playing high status to the chair by adopting an authoritative posture or demeanour. This allows you to get comfortable with expressing high status without a prying audience. Repeat with low status.

Understanding Titles and Status

Often our environment and the people around us influence our status. In most agile teams I encounter, job titles and roles can imply an inherent status that others resist challenging. These job titles are shown in the table below in Figure 4.4. **Title-implied status can create an unsafe working environment where developers feel too inferior to take responsibility or make decisions and managers feel empowered to make commitments on behalf of other people.**

Implied High-Status Job Roles	Implied Low-Status Job Roles
Chief Architect	Quality Assurance (QA)
Project Manager	Manual Tester
Design Authority	Technical Writer
Lead Developer	Junior Developer
Product Owner	Proxy Product Owner

Figure 4.4 Examples of high- and low-status job titles in software organisations

Agile frameworks sometimes also have titles that seem to imply status. One example from Scrum is the role of ScrumMaster. Some people I have spoken to have a real issue with the name itself, as "master" could imply high status or some kind of god-like figure. Interestingly, Ken Schwaber once told me he conceived the name to deter managers and executives (implied high-status roles) from taking the position on the team, and therefore using that role to control people rather than support them.

To combat title-implied status, some Scrum teams I have worked with in the past have attempted to replace the term "ScrumMaster" with a lower-status role name, such as Scrum Monkey, Scrum Secretary, or even Scrum Bitch. However, I would suggest this is lowering the status too much, thereby devaluing the role completely and rejecting its purpose. Better examples I have heard used include Team Enabler, Whitewater

River Guide, Invisible Gorilla Watcher, Über Facilitator, Team Whisperer, and Team System Mirror. All of these titles have lower status relative to "Scrum*Master*" but still convey the value the ScrumMaster brings to the team and organisation.

Whatever your role, and whatever name you choose for that role, be aware of how your title might affect your own status response or the responses of others to you. If your title carries a high-status implication, make an intentional choice to lower your status when working with others. Conversely, if your title seems to be more low status, occasionally choose a higher-status response. You might be surprised at how much the behaviour of the people around you changes when you do so.

When it comes to leading an agile team, whether as a ScrumMaster or coach or as a manager, the goal should be to motivate the team in any way you can – not by controlling them, but by *enabling* them. The agile manifesto principles advise that we should do the following:

> *"Build projects around motivated individuals.*
> *Give them the environment and support they need,*
> *and trust them to get the job done."*[6]

In a leadership position, if the goal is to support, enable, and ultimately trust the individuals in our team, we need to be prepared to lower our status, even if our job title might imply a higher status.

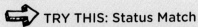 **TRY THIS: Status Match**
During a conversation where you feel the status gap is growing, make a conscious effort to match the status of the other person. This can be as simple as mirroring their body language or demeanour.[7]

Playing Team Status to Artefacts

If you tried the status chair exercise I suggested earlier, you have an idea about how individuals can play status not only to other people but also to the objects they see and use. **Some work-related artefacts are easily misinterpreted as high-status objects, owned by people in perceived higher-status roles.**

In traditional software project management, almost all the artefacts designed to support the process are created and maintained by those in management roles, thus increasing the perception that they are high-status objects belonging to high-status people. Gantt charts, status reports, and risk or issue logs are all artefacts that fall into this category, and are typically only discussed and debated during management meetings.

In contrast, agile software development aims to spread the responsibility of project management among those who are leading and those who are delivering the projects. Hence, the development team has more responsibility for maintaining project-related artefacts.

An example of this is the burndown chart, an artefact designed to enable teams to self-regulate progress within the iteration. This is an artefact that the development team is meant to own and update, but often when I talk to the teams themselves, they don't update it because they perceive "someone in charge" looks after that. This sometimes happens when someone with a high-status title inadvertently assumes a high-status position over these artefacts (sometimes by something as subtle as keeping the burndown too close to one person's desk or by a ScrumMaster who "helps" the team by updating the burndown when they forget). Unsurprisingly, agile software tools can have an interesting effect on status within a team too. If these tools are largely being used, viewed, and updated by those people regarded as high status, those with lower status will take less interest or ownership of them. **When high-status individuals assume ownership of an object or indeed an agile artefact, even unintentionally, they can force lower-status team members away from it.**

The artefact that teams tend to feel most belongs to them is the task board. No matter which agile process you follow, members of the team will be more involved and engaged if they use a physical task board that displays the tasks they agree need to be completed to make their commitment a success. The team feels ownership when they have created the content and contributed to its structure and purpose. That's the key to matching both of these artefacts to the team's default status – the team should own them and feel responsible for updating them. To encourage this, ask the team to create their own task board – one with the information they need to monitor their own progress towards delivery. Ask them to think of similar actions that they could take to feel similar responsibility for the burndown or any other constituent items they need to maintain. In a recent coaching engagement, I saw a team transformed when they rubbed out the marker lines that their boss had drawn on "his" backlog whiteboard. This one seemingly innocuous act empowered them to claim ownership of one of the project-related artefacts.

Can you think of any examples of artefacts you have to work with that you or others "play status" with? Luckily this is quite easy to adjust, once you realise you are doing it. While working at Nokia, I used to make a conscious effort to stand behind flipcharts or task boards during meetings. Not because I was shy or retiring, but because I wanted my team to use the objects directly, rather than use them through me.

Coaching Using Status

As an agile coach myself, I have a hard challenge in using status effectively when I am coaching teams. I believe a good agile coach is one who serves their client or team by enabling them to grow and gain enough confidence to continue the agile journey unassisted, and therefore my status as a coach often starts high but then decreases slowly over time.

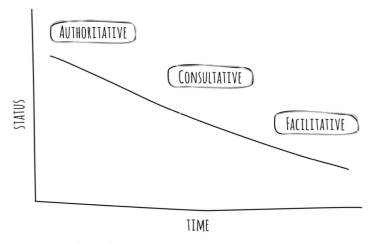

Figure 4.5 Ideally, a coach's overall status will decrease over time

For example, when I am asked to come in and coach new teams (or teams that are less confident with an agile approach to their work) I may be required to take a higher-status, more authoritative approach, in order to lead those teams into the unknown. In other words, at first I will need to direct meetings, educate stakeholders, and offer guidance, as the lower-status team members will look to me to take the agile initiative. As the coaching engagement progresses, I adjust my status to only offer advice on more of a consultative basis. This could include making suggestions on how certain processes could be improved.

My aim, over time, is to lower my status in relationship to those stakeholders down to a facilitative style, whereby my role is to support those responsible for continuing the agile adoption internally as the agile principles become embedded in the company culture (see Figure 4.5). I want to provide just enough support to empower those people to propose new ideas or take ownership of a challenging scenario without my permission or counsel.

One of the best ways agile coaches can lower their status is to ask more questions rather than provide more answers. But, achieving a lower status when doing this, without appearing docile and apathetic, is not easy.

"How can I help you achieve that?"

"What data can I provide to highlight this problem?"

"What impediment can I remove to aid progress here?"

These are all examples of what agile coaches can say to lower their status enough to enable others to move forward under their own steam. And the common denominator is "enabling". **Good agile coaches know how to lower their status just enough to enable clients to move forward for themselves.**

Keep in mind, though, that there may be times where an agile coach will need to raise their status, for example to protect the integrity of the iteration from a pushy customer who is attempting to crowbar extra work in. Trying to squeeze in additional work introduces risk because it jeopardises the team's current commitment, potentially lowering the quality of the product the team delivers. In cases like these, the coach should confront the customer and present them with another offer – a high-status response. **Agile coaches, therefore, should vary their status depending on the situation and the relationship.**

Collaborate Using Status

While an agile coach has to master status better than most, all members of an agile team stand to benefit from an understanding of status and how to alter it to best fit the situation. Improv author and teacher Keith Johnstone encourages his students to become comfortable with playing both high and low status on stage. This makes them more adaptable as actors, and more capable of producing engaging and interesting scenes for the audience.[8] **Agile teams should also play with status – a process that can allow collaboration to occur more naturally.**

The first thing to understand is how status affects an individual's decision to accept or block offers from others. In improvisational theatre, low-status players are more likely to accept the offer another player makes. At the same time, high-status players are more likely to resist or block offers, unless they feel they can control them.[9]

These same dynamics play out in agile teams. Though many team members are open to the ideas of their teammates, I have seen many lead developers (playing high status) exercise their authority over junior developers (playing low status) by immediately rejecting or *blocking* their new ideas or suggestions. Equally, I can recall several instances of low-status team members jumping on the first *offer* that a team member playing high status has suggested. Interestingly, in some teams I have worked with, team members have used their perceived lower status to avoid the responsibilities that an agile team member should embrace. For instance, these team members might perpetuate the myth that only those in management roles can update agile artefacts such as the burndown chart or only the product owner can add items to the product backlog.

To collaborate more effectively, agile teams must learn how to break out of these status tendencies and habits. Becoming comfortable with playing status is one way to reduce the status gaps in a business setting. The status games at the end of this chapter are great ways for agile teams to firstly become aware of status, but then start to understand how team members can collaborate more readily by being prepared to change their own status in relation to their fellow team members.

Change Using Status

Students of improvisational theatre learn to play status on stage not just to create relationships between characters, but also to change those relationships to generate interesting storylines and move the action forward. During an improvised scene, an audience is captivated when a status switch occurs – the maid who purposely spills a glass of wine over her employer, or the boss who bursts into tears as the worker comforts him.

In adopting an agile approach, teams accept the inevitability that change is expected. In software certainly, many customers don't know how to explain what they want until they see something that they *don't* want; therefore, they often change their descriptions of *what* to build (their requirements) as the project progresses. Add to that the endless variability in software design and technology – the vast number of potential languages, frameworks, methods, and protocols to choose from in order to create software products – and the likelihood is that teams could change *how* they build the solution as well.

Humans have a hard time accepting change. Human brains find change innately difficult to compute. The human brain is one big hard drive that has been storing life's data since the moment we were born. People's reactions, moods, and responses are tuned to their own life experiences – to what has made them feel happy or sad in the past. Like a computer, the brain likes to build on previous examples and experiences to determine how to tackle problems and situations. Change challenges these patterns, and as a result people tend not to trust new data that they can't prove, causing them to act irrationally and try to prevent that change.

Change cannot be forced onto others. Before individuals can accept change in their projects and processes they must first accept change within themselves. Sometimes a person's natural preference of high or low status, or indeed a status implied by a job title, can make accepting that change much more challenging.

If, however, individuals can observe and rationalise how their own responses vary depending on the behaviour of those around them – and why it is sometimes advantageous to deliberately go against their instinctive reactions – they can become more comfortable with embracing change both personally and professionally.

Can you think of something you can do today that might help you be more open to change?

PLAY
STATUS
GAMES

Status Games

These status games are designed to help agile teams recognise status behaviours and then subsequently learn how they can become more playful in changing status. As such, I recommend playing these games in the sequence that follows.

THE DINNER PARTY[10]

Players	Timebox	Energy Level	Individual	Team	Visual	Verbal	Physical	Scenario
5–9	15 mins	***	****	*	***	****	***	Anytime

Synopsis

In this game, various players take on different status behaviours while at an imaginary dinner party. One team member will play host. This game allows the players to consciously see the effect of status signals and how we react to them. This game is a good introduction to identifying status because the facilitator, rather than the players, defines the behaviour.

Script

The game is best played in a large room with no tables or chairs. Split the players into two groups. Arbitrarily identify one player who will play the party host, but don't disclose this to the group just yet.

FACILITATOR: "We are going to imagine we are at a dinner party where [player's name] is the host."

Point to one of the two groups – this group will be using a high-status signal.

FACILITATOR: "This group will attempt to keep their head perfectly still while they talk to other people at the party."

Point to the other group – this group will be taking on a low-status signal.

FACILITATOR: "Whereas this group will attempt to blink much more frequently than you would normally. Aim for two to three blinks per second."

Ensure both groups understand the desired behaviours and kick-start the dinner party into action.

FACILITATOR: "OK, the party is underway. Meet people and have fun!"

Side Coaching

"Mingle to meet new people! Be nice and friendly!"

"Say hello to the host!"

Shift

After five minutes, switch the behaviours between the groups.

Speculation

"How did your behaviour affect your confidence?"

"How did your behaviour affect others around you?"

"Who did you connect with at the party? Why?"

"Who did you avoid at the party? Why?"

Suggestions

Repeat with other status signals, such as touching your face (low status) and pausing before answering questions (high status).

Try the same exercise with "blind" status signals (i.e. don't make public which status you are using).

STATUS CORRIDOR[11]

Players	Timebox	Energy Level	Individual	Team	Visual	Verbal	Physical	Scenario
4–16	15 mins	***	****	***	***	****	***	Anytime

Synopsis

This game allows players to play status within the relative safety of improvising short, three-line scenes with a partner. This is another good game to help players differentiate between a high- and low-status response.

Script

This game requires an open space where the players can stand and move freely. Ask the group to arrange themselves in two parallel lines, facing each other. Should you have an odd number, the odd one out can help the facilitator by providing the suggestions for the game.

The facilitator should address the group as two sides of a corridor.

FACILITATOR: "We are going to create very short scenes that only contain three lines of dialogue. If you are standing on *this* side [pointing to one side of the corridor] you should play a high status in the scene. Those on the other side [pointing to opposite side] will play a low-status player in the scene. Remember, the scene is only three lines of dialogue, and then we move on to the next pairs of players in the line."

As a facilitator, you will have to give some context to the scene for each pair of players. This can be as simple as a location (e.g. a hospital) or emotion (e.g. jealousy), or for more inexperienced players more detailed scenarios (e.g. schoolteacher telling off a naughty pupil).

Start the first line with the high-status player, cross over to the low-status response, and back to the high-status player to complete the scene.

Move down the line, changing the context each time.

Side Coaching

"It doesn't have to be funny or original!"

"Just be obvious. The status makes it interesting!"

Shift

When all the players have played their scenes, reverse the status. You can also switch who starts the scene by allowing the low-status player to speak first and last.

Speculation

"Where were the largest status changes?"

"What made the most interesting scenes?"

"Which side of the corridor were you most comfortable on? Why?"

Suggestions

If players enjoy the acting, increase to five or six lines of dialogue, and switch the status halfway through the scene (after the third line for instance).

STATUS STAND-UP

Players	Timebox	Energy Level	Individual	Team	Visual	Verbal	Physical	Scenario
5–9	15 mins	**	****	*	***	****	***	Daily Stand-up

Synopsis

Once the team understands how to play status a little more, we can play some status games in the daily stand-up. By changing their status consciously on a daily basis, the team will be able to change status to collaborate more unconsciously between those meetings.

Script

Each of the players will determine the status of the next player by the flip of a coin.

FACILITATOR: "During today's daily stand-up we are going to adjust our behaviours based on the flip of a coin. If it's heads, the next player must play a higher status than the previous player – even if that player is already playing a high status. If it's tails, the next player must play a lower status, even if that player is already playing a low status."

After each update, the player firstly names who will speak next, and then flips the coin to determine how the status will change.

It's quite possible that the status could become extremely high or extremely low – this is especially fun where people are playing a status they are not naturally suited to.

Speculation

"What made this more or less engaging for you?"

"Did anyone find his or her behaviour uncomfortable?"

"Did anyone find his or her natural behaviour came out?"

Suggestions

The same random flip of a coin could determine the status of responses in other meetings such as planning sessions or retrospectives.

SMELLY, SEXY, STUPID[12]

Players	Timebox	Energy Level	Individual	Team	Visual	Verbal	Physical	Scenario
4–10	15 mins	****	****	***	***	****	***	Anytime

Synopsis

This game allows the team to observe more natural status responses because the players themselves determine how they will interact with other players. There is a real skill in noticing and adjusting to very subtle changes in status.

Script

The game needs four players and enough space to act out a short scene. Feel free to use chairs and tables to add authenticity. The remaining players serve as the audience.

FACILITATOR: "The four of you will now imagine you are at a party, and one of you is the host. Decide among you who the host will be."

FACILITATOR: "All four of you will now make a judgement about each of your fellow party-goers. You need to imagine that one of them is smelly, one of them is sexy, and the remaining one is stupid. The catch is that you don't tell those players what you've decided their attribute is. That means that as a group, you could determine that the same player is sexy, smelly, and stupid, if each of you assigns a different attribute to that individual."

Allow the party to start and watch the awkward encounters when a player who is regarded as smelly finds their opposite number sexy. Also watch what happens when a player someone thinks is smelly is considered sexy by another player.

Allow the scene to run for five minutes, and then stop the players. Tell them each to reveal who they chose as the smelly one, the sexy one, and so on. This reminds the players that it was just a game, and not real life.

Side Coaching

You may need to re-emphasise that the players are all friends. They wouldn't want to offend each other. This encourages the players to make the status signals more subtle.

Shift

Change the players with four observers and mix the groups. The observing team members have an important role in observing the scene. Many interactions will be taking place at one time, so encourage observers to focus on watching one player at a time.

Speculation

"Did the players work out who liked whom? And who didn't?"

"Did the observing team members work it out?"

"What made the relationships obvious?"

"How did the players move around the stage?"

"What signals did the other players give you?"

Suggestions

Experiment with different attributes at the party such as someone who is:
- nosy;
- hilarious;
- irritating;
- boring;
- delicate;
- rude; or
- ugly.

I QUIT... DUMBASS!

Players	Timebox	Energy Level	Individual	Team	Visual	Verbal	Physical	Scenario
5–9	15 mins	**	****	***	*	****	**	Anytime

Synopsis

This game teaches teams how playing with insults can help them play with status more effectively (i.e. high-status players have their status challenged by lower-status players who insult them). I would suggest this game only be played with teams who have established a comfortable level of safety (See Chapter 1, "Safety") and are prepared to play this game in the spirit intended.

Script

The players will need paper and pens to write down suggestions for the game.

FACILITATOR: "I want you to imagine the worst boss you could ever have. Imagine that your boss made your life hell by hassling you and making you work long, painful hours on horrible, stressful projects. Luckily you just won the lottery and are walking into your boss's office to hand in your resignation. You have one final chance to insult your boss as you leave, but you must frame this insult by exclaiming 'I quit...' and then adding a playful insult, such as 'Dumbass!' or something tame enough not to offend your fellow players."

FACILITATOR: "On your paper, write down any names you would love to call your fictional boss at that point."

You may need to set the correct tone by using other examples that emphasise playful insults rather than offensive ones. If in doubt, blend an animal with a body part or function such as monkey-face, camel-breath, or bug-eyes.

Allow five minutes for the team to write down their ideas in private.

FACILITATOR: "Now pass your paper to someone else in the group who will screen anything too offensive. I'd like you to then shout out any words you would like to use in the game, and leave out any that you don't like."

Write down the words the players shout out on a large piece of flipchart paper in the room.

Two volunteers will now play a simple scene unrelated to the boss/lottery scene you described earlier. One example might be buying an item from a shop, where one player is the customer and the other is the shopkeeper.

FACILITATOR: "During this conversation, when you speak you need to add one of the insults from the flipchart to the end of your sentence, such as 'Can I buy some cheese please, knucklehead?' The other player's response must also end with an insult from the list."

The observing team members will enjoy the slapstick element to the conversation as the transaction quickly descends into a playful argument.

Side Coaching

"What did she just call you?!? That's outrageous!"

Point out the audacity of the name-calling and encourage the players to react realistically to the insults.

Shift

Switch the players with other team members to allow others to give and receive the insults. Restart the scene if necessary when this happens.

Speculation

"How did you respond to being insulted?"

"How did it feel to insult someone else?"

"What made the scene more interesting to the audience?"

"How did the reactions differ from player to player?"

"How was the status of the players changed in this exercise?"

Suggestions

Add a third player into the scene. Players must direct the insults to a specific player, who then responds with an insult to one of the other two players.

Establish a status gap before the scene starts, such as an army sergeant addressing a new recruit or a parent addressing their teenage offspring.

SENSITIVITY

An improviser stands alone on stage and asks the audience for
a location where she can set her scene.

The audience offers "a church". The improviser gladly accepts and
begins to create the scene.

She hunches her shoulders slightly, folding her arms as if she feels the cold
air around her. She walks across the stage and kneels at an altar, bowing her
head and signing a cross on her chest. She stands and then walks over to light
a candle.

Without a single line of dialogue, the scene is now set.
All that remains is for her fellow improvisers to accept
her invitation and join her on stage…

SENSITIVITY

After researching and watching some of the great improvisers, I remain in awe of their seemingly effortless ability to tune in and create amazing scenes in collaboration with their fellow performers. When we watch a performance, we may rate performers based on their ability to make us laugh, tell a good story, or play a role or persona well. But among their peers, great improvisers are the actors who make *other* actors look good by virtue of their sensitivity.

Google defines sensitivity as "1. Quick to detect or respond to slight changes, signals, or influences. 2. Having and displaying a quick and delicate appreciation of others' feelings."[1] There is no doubt that in this chapter's opening scene, the improviser displays extraordinary sensitivity with her nearly instantaneous yet fully developed response to the signal, a church. And anyone who has ever witnessed a live improv performance can attest to how sensitive each actor is to the action on stage.

A high level of sensitivity is just as important in an agile team as it is in improv – and is just as appreciated by your fellow teammates as it is by an improviser's fellow actors. Developing this vital trait, however, may not come as naturally as you might think. Becoming and remaining keenly sensitive requires continuous practice and improvement.

This final chapter looks at the critical skills that an improviser has to develop in order to foster the level of sensitivity necessary to make an improvised performance seem effortless. It also explores how those same skills are vital for members of an agile team (and indeed in life). These skills are selflessness, listening, observation, recollection, and emotional awareness.

Selflessness

"Real living is living for others"
Bruce Lee[2]

People are selfless when they think of other people before they think of themselves. The best improvisers (those that other improvisers clamber to work with) enable their fellow improvisers to look good. As Keith Johnstone explained at a recent workshop, "If everyone wants to work with you, you may be a good improviser, even if you think you are not".[3] The skills of in-demand improvisers are just as high as their peers on stage, but they also excel at allowing others to succeed, even if that requires stepping out of the limelight themselves.

The best improvisers understand that they may have to abandon their own interpretation of a character, or their own spin on the storyline, multiple times within a single scene or story. Yet they do this without remorse or disappointment, because they trust that their colleagues on stage will build on these moments and find ways to do the same for them later in the scene. In contrast, improvisers whose aim is to always look funny or come up with the most original idea tend to find themselves in scenes where the actors appear disconnected with each other or are left following disjointed storylines. As such, the best improvisers are selfless – **and being selfless involves sacrifice.**

But how does being selfless apply to agile teams? I heard a great story from Richard Sheridan, one of the keynote speakers at the New Orleans Global Scrum Gathering 2014, who gave an inspirational experience report on his company's adoption of agile techniques. When asked about the recruitment process for new developers, he explained how after an initial, more traditional interview, his company assesses the candidate's ability to build software in a team environment. The candidates are split into pairs and then told they will be judged only on their ability to "make their partner look good".[4]

I connected with Richard's case study not only from the application of improvisation to their employee selection process, but also in how software organisations have historically appraised their staff. In my experience, organisations typically reward employees for meeting arbitrary objectives and succeeding as individuals, rather than creating something innovative as a team through supporting and enabling others. These individual reward and recognition systems lead team members and employees to believe that stretching themselves brings career progression and rewards within the company. This play-to-win mentality leads to individualistic thinking, where people protect their own interests rather than maximising the opportunities that others may have.

An unwillingness to admit weakness or failure ultimately results in an unsafe corporate environment, with very little teamwork or creativity.

If, on the other hand, companies remove the pressure to be better than their colleagues (by playing to win), and instead reward team members who allow others to carry the baton, they will create a safer, more collaborative, and more enjoyable working environment.

 TRY THIS: Selfless Act
Can you recall a recent business situation where someone put you before himself or herself? What were the consequences?

Listening

> *"Listening is more important than talking.*
> *Just listen to people and react to what they are saying"*
> Jimmy Fallon[5]

According to coaching guru Julie Starr, people adopt four levels of listening, depending on the depth of the conversation they are having:

- **Cosmetic Listening:** listening while involved in another activity, such as listening to the radio while driving. Those listening at this level while in a conversation might nod or add listening noises, but really are just waiting for a gap so they can take their turn.
- **Conversational Listening:** participating in a conversation but conscious of our surroundings and other distractions. At this level, people focus on what others are saying, but are also often thinking about what they have said, and what they might say next.
- **Active Listening:** focusing on the speaker, making a concerted effort to listen, processing the information, and understanding what is being said. Active listeners may ask clarifying questions or play back what they have heard.
- **Deep Listening:** focusing to the point where we are unaware of our self or our surroundings. When people listen at this level, any thoughts of their own responses will come after the speaker has finished speaking.[6]

For an improviser, listening is paramount to the flow of a performance. If there were a script, actors could practise their lines in isolation before a performance and simply speak up at the appropriate time after the curtain goes up. Without a script, however, the actors must be listening for offers at all times (see Chapter 2, "Spontaneity", for more on offers).

When improvising on stage, the actors are constantly varying the depth of listening they apply. For instance, when gathering suggestions from the audience, they are listening at a more conversational level; improv troupes must stay in direct contact with the audience in order to deliver a good show. Yet when performing a scene, the same actors are fully immersed in deep listening. **If they are not actively listening for offers, they may**

stifle the flow of the storyline and others' creativity. The ability to alter listening depth is often what separates a great improviser from an average one.

For an agile team, the importance of listening is underlined by the sixth principle of the agile manifesto, which states:

> *"The most efficient and effective method of conveying information to and within a development team is face-to-face conversation."*[7]

Although this statement could imply that conversational listening is the goal for the team, **I believe the ability to vary the depth of listening is as essential for members of an agile team as it is to improvisers.**

Agile team members can increase their depth of listening purely through practice, just as improvisers would in every performance. And luckily, an agile team has built-in opportunities to practise better listening. The primary purpose of the 15-minute daily stand-up (or daily scrum), for example, is to focus on listening rather than speaking. The rule I pass on to the teams I coach and teach is to take one minute to speak and the other 14 minutes to listen.

⟹ TRY THIS: Blind Stand-up
Ask attendees to close their eyes during a regular daily stand-up. Deprived of sight, attendees should focus more on listening.

Adding constraints to how you speak can make listening a more interesting activity. I can remember one of the most absorbing daily stand-ups I attended, where I asked each of the team members to impersonate someone else in the team when they spoke. Other team members immediately became more engaged in listening to *what* was being said, as well as *how* it was being said. Deep listening in these types of meetings also allows all team members to listen to what *hasn't* been said, rather than what has, which can help team members identify issues or fears that haven't yet surfaced.

 TRY THIS: Toothless Stand-up
Ask attendees to speak at the daily stand-up without showing their teeth, by keeping them covered only with their lips. Apart from being fun, masking words encourages others to focus more on listening.

Purely through practising deeper listening, even if it's just for 15 minutes during the daily stand-up, anyone can contribute more to the conversations and collaboration that need to occur during the working day.

Observation

"Spotting the aberrations, spotting the mistakes, looking for
the little unusual thing, that's often where a fruitful future lies."
Richard Vranch[8]

Wherever you are right now, I'd like you to put this book down (just for ten seconds) and look around. Try to notice something that you haven't noticed before. It doesn't have to be anything extraordinary or life-enhancing, just something you hadn't noticed before you read this paragraph.

I did the same, and I noticed an old receipt behind my monitor, dated November 2014. From reading it, I remember the meal I ate at The Old Crown, in Birmingham, England, just prior to talking at the Heart of England User Group. I ate ham, eggs, and chips that evening while I sat and chatted with the group organisers before the event began.

What you observe might not always be profound, but my point is that **it's very easy to blot out elements of the environment that you see every day, purely because you aren't looking for them.** You can repeat the same exercise with the focus on listening too, by closing your eyes and trying to hear things around you that you weren't hearing before.

In Chapter 1, "Safety", I talked about the value of slowing down. I discussed how Guy Claxton's theory suggests that the default speed (d-mode) of intelligence is one built on logical thought, where we are attempting to solve a problem in the most efficient and timely manner. As society puts a high value on our default mode, we tend to value explanations and solutions over observations and problems. Hence, the speed at which we are expected to process questions and find answers leads us to "see" without really "looking".[9]

Taking more time to observe our situation can help prepare us for tackling those situations.

> **TRY THIS: Eyes Wide Open**
> Purposefully widen your eyes (for as long as possible without causing pain!) during a team discussion or retrospective. See if it widens your perspective on the discussion or possible outcome.

In sports psychology, top athletes practise visualisation as part of their training, by imagining themselves achieving their goals under extreme pressure. Scientific research suggests that this type of "visual rehearsal" actually triggers neural responses, which serve as a mental blueprint that can actually improve future performance. High-profile athletes such as Jonny Wilkinson (rugby), Jessica Ennis-Hill (heptathlon), and Andy Murray (tennis) have all benefited from imagining themselves in high-pressure situations or intimidating environments to prepare their body and mind for an upcoming event.[10]

Improvisers don't just listen for audible cues – they also look for offers that might be communicated by changes in body language. Subtle changes in status, for instance, are often visual offers rather than verbal ones (see Chapter 4, "Status"). Several improvisation games use mime as a means to exchange offers. Mime games are a great way to develop observational skills, and to learn to collaborate without necessarily using sound. Miming actions encourages individuals to be more specific and obvious with their offers. This gives others a better chance of connecting to and progressing the action.

Watching trained improvisers waiting off stage for a chance to come on stage highlights how keen their powers of observation really are. During a well-known improv game called Freeze-Tag, two improvisers act out a scene until an offstage improviser calls "freeze". The onstage actors must freeze in their current positions until the new actor "tags" one of them, which is the frozen actor's cue to leave the stage. The new actor must assume the body position of the actor s/he replaced, and construct a new scene from that point. To do this successfully, the offstage actors must be constantly looking for non-verbal offers to accept in the form of interesting body positions.

 TRY THIS: Mime Stand-up
Ask attendees to mime their updates at the daily stand-up. Allow them to point to people, tasks, and artefacts. Encourage observers to narrate the mime to confirm the information has been correctly understood.

Strengthening observation skills can help an agile team to communicate and collaborate more effectively on a daily basis. Firstly, when individuals consciously observe others during conversations, they are better able to pick up the non-verbal *status* signals (see Chapter 4, "Status") that others are offering, thus allowing the team to collaborate more freely. But secondly, I believe conditioning team members to observe their surroundings more closely on a daily basis can help individuals, teams, and entire organisations inspect and adapt their processes and behaviours on many levels.

For example, once when I was a ScrumMaster of a team, I took time each day purely to sit at my desk and watch the team at work. Not because I was nosy or controlling, but because I wanted to observe their behaviours. One day I noticed a team member, working alone at his desk, stop, push his keyboard away, and put his head in his hands. When he looked up, his eyes were red and watery, as if crying. He sniffed quietly, dried his eyes, and carried on with his work. Later that morning, I stopped him in a quiet corridor and told him what I saw. He told me that he was going through some difficult personal issues at home and was having trouble concentrating in the office. After some discussion we agreed that he should take some time off. On his return he thanked me for confronting him with those issues. Had I not taken the time to observe the signal, that reflection might not have occurred.

As an agile coach, I encounter many organisational foibles and process shortcuts that my clients have been living with for months, even years, but no longer notice or see. By far the most frequently occurring dysfunction is where there is too much work in progress relative to the amount of people available to work on it. Lean principles advise that partially done work increases both waste and financial risk, yet many of my clients still take on more work than they can comfortably handle, which leads to an environment where wasteful context-switching and multitasking is commonplace.

Sometimes my role as an agile coach is simply to observe and expose the dysfunctions that my client has become blind to.

One of the best ways to focus more fully on noticing non-verbal cues is through an improv game called Gibberish. Originally a creation of Keith Johnstone, this advanced game asks improvisers to converse in a fictitious foreign language. Johnstone found that this helped to create a safer environment for his students (the actors feel less worried about what to say), thereby increasing their ability to listen closely and interact non-verbally.[11]

Figure 5.1 Talking in gibberish

Talking in gibberish is challenging but can be fun to try with an agile team. On second thoughts, most software development teams I've met usually talk in gibberish to each other on a daily basis anyway!

Recollection

If we practise visualisation and observation more readily, it aids our ability to retain and store information. As a child, when I lost something at home, my mother would always ask, "Where did you last see it?" Although her question was always predictably frustrating, it was the right question to ask. People's memories are aided by the visual images they capture.[12] I know, for example, that if I take more time to capture and study the observation in real time, I stand a better chance of remembering it at a later date.

To an improviser, the ability to recall what has gone before is paramount to creating an interesting story. Their ability to reincorporate the past (see Chapter 3, "Storytelling") will increase if they can listen, observe, retain, and recall previous offers. The members of an audience will delight in a performance from improvisers who can reintroduce old offers and connect them with the storyline.

In agile development, a team's capacity to recall previous data and knowledge is tested on a regular basis. In a daily stand-up meeting, team members need to recall what they did yesterday. For those team members who have a short memory, the task board can be used to prompt them. In a retrospective, however, the team needs to recall what happened over the last two, three, or maybe even four weeks, which can be a tough task. Though product backlog, task boards, and burndowns are great for jogging memory, I have found that teams can retain and recall more data if they use more of their brains to store it at the time. While memory can't be exercised exactly like a muscle, people can learn how to organise information in their brains in order to improve how their own memories operate.[13]

A survey conducted by the BBC in 2006 revealed that smaller amounts or "chunks" of data tend to be easier to remember – another benefit of the daily stand-up.[14] For me personally, I store information such as workshop attendees' names through repetition or cramming. Though this works well for a two-day training course, I can't retain that data for long periods of time. For long-term data storage, I use imagery. I can remember a phone number if I remember the colour or position of the paper it's written on, or the style or colour of the handwriting or font. Looking at a photograph helps me remember particular events or emotions I experienced, and often triggers other memories as a result. I frequently use photographs taken by team members during retrospectives I am leading.

 TRY THIS: Words to Remember
Ask team members to agree on a single word that summarises the day's events before they leave the office. Write down all those words at the start of a retrospective to help the team remember what happened on that particular day during the iteration.

Emotional Awareness

Audience members expect actors to demonstrate a range of emotions. Many critics assess an individual's acting performance on not just the lines that were delivered, but also by the emotional connection the actor made with the role or character.

People's ability to monitor their own emotions, as well as the emotions of those around them (their sensitivity to their own and to others' feelings), is valuable in any situation, in or out of a work environment. This ability is called emotional intelligence, and is connected to greater mental health, exemplary job performance, and more potential leadership skills.[15]

Due to the short-lived nature of their performances, improv actors connect with both the audience and the other actors very quickly, and often create offers simply by showing or playing emotions. Being aware of how emotions change depending on perspective also helps the actors more easily switch status, which can deepen many scenes. A classic short-form improv game called Emotions involves audience-led rapid-fire suggestions, where the actors will create a single scene but alter the story as they assume a variety of suggested emotions.

We can use these types of games and exercises firstly to increase awareness of the different types of emotions that exist, and secondly to understand how emotions change a person's thoughts and interactions.

I once used a variation of the dysfunctional daily stand-up game to help a team understand some of the emotions they were experiencing (or in some cases ignoring) on a daily basis.[16] I gave the attendees index cards. Each index card had a different emotion for the speaker to show when giving an update:

- apathy;
- paranoia;
- aggression;
- sarcasm;
- courage; or
- confusion.

Despite some early animosity, the team relished the chance to act in the relative safety of their daily meeting. But the most telling part of the exercise was that the team started to call out some of the behaviours that their peers had been guilty of in previous meetings! Only when their peers mimicked those same behaviours did some team members start to ask themselves, "Do I really do that?" **Self-awareness is the first step to increasing emotional intelligence. Sometimes deliberately *playing* an emotion is a safe way to make that breakthrough.**

Being "In the Moment"

"People think it's hard work? It's no work.
If you follow the process, and remain awake, it just happens."
Lee Simpson[17]

Improvisers place all of these sensitivity skills under the umbrella of *being in the moment*. This is a state in which they are engaged and tuned into the other actors, and are ready to perform. Performers are in the moment when they are completely immersed in the scene – in a state of increased sensitivity. Many memorable moments in cinematic history have come from movies where the director has let the cameras roll while the actors have improvised their lines.[18] Martin Scorsese, the Hollywood director responsible for many Oscar-nominated films (such as *The Departed*, *Gangs of New York*, and *The Wolf of Wall Street*), is well-known for leaving gaps in his script that are retrospectively filled after the actors have improvised dialogues on camera.

An example is actor Robert De Niro's performance in Scorsese's film *Taxi Driver* (1976), summed up in his now infamous line, "Are you talking to me?" This was part of a monologue left unscripted by Scorsese, allowing De Niro to improvise while deep in character.[19]

On an agile team, all of the creativity the team members can access already exists. There are countless ideas and offers all around waiting for someone to accept them, but the hardest job anyone has is to focus on them. In today's technological age, the background noise is deafening. Mobile phones, the internet, instant messaging, video conferences, and social media are so ubiquitous that people are saturated with information. **As such, I believe people have become desensitised.** To counteract this, teams have to consciously kick-start these skills back into life, and condition themselves every day to remain truly "in the moment".

Thinking "Inside the Box"

The phrases I hear a lot regarding creative thinking include blue-sky and outside-the-box thinking. What I have learned and applied from improvisational theatre is almost exactly the opposite. **Adding constraints to a process, choosing to remain inside the box, can enhance creativity, not restrict it.** Having boundaries gives people focus, but only if they recondition themselves to be open to change within those limits. Any project will undoubtedly have some constraints too. An agile approach may well have boundaries around project length or budget, understanding of the market or technology, acceptance criteria for requirements, or the skill and experience of those in the team. But those same project boundaries can boost creativity, if teams can adjust the way they operate within them.

The members of an agile team will create more when it feels like they are playing. But individuals will only play when they feel safe. In this book, I have consciously named those playing games as "players" with the hope that the focus is to play, rather than to win. **Safety** comes when team members know that they can call on others for help, but also when they know that accepting failure and slowing down can have a positive effect on a team's willingness to experiment.

If agile teams can establish a level of safety, they can start to challenge how they filter their own ideas in order to increase their **spontaneity**. Once people get past how an idea will be perceived, they can be content with being unoriginal and obvious, and generate more *offers* for others to build on, rather than closing down suggestions or adding *blocks* to protect their own interests.

The art of **storytelling** can help engage an agile team in the narrative of product creation. Good stories with simple storylines allow teams to empathise and connect with their customers. Connecting story elements together allows the team to see their product designs emerge. And don't underestimate the sense of fulfilment a team gains from seeing their work complete and the story come to a satisfying end.

The **status** people play at work affects how they collaborate with others. Once people understand their own natural preference for either high or low status and how the status people play affects their ability to accept an offer or block progress, they can learn to change their own behaviours to effect change in others.

The degree to which team members take on these principles of improvisation is determined by their **sensitivity**. Individuals need to remember that they can still look good by making others look good. They need to practise deeper listening and understand that how people store events can help them recall them more readily at later points. By conditioning themselves to establishing and maintaining a level of focus around these softer skills, teams remain more alive and open to change, even (and especially) if there are constraints they must work within.

My hope is that this book, my *offer* if you like, will help.

I wonder if your sensitivity is already heightened as a result of reading this book?

I set out writing this book as an experiment. The first part of the experiment was to exercise my own writing creativity under constraints. The book itself is a constraint, of course, as you will only hear your own inner voice reading these words instead of mine. But I wanted to add more constraints to challenge my imaginative brain, a process that improvisers seem to flourish within.

The simple constraints I applied to this book all involve the letter S.

Firstly, I applied the constraint that within this book, all of the five principal chapters must start with the letter S:

- safety;
- spontaneity;
- storytelling;
- status; and
- sensitivity.

I applied the same constraint to the game description headings:

- synopsis;
- script;
- shift;
- side coaching;
- speculation; and
- suggestions.

But I wanted to stretch my creativity further. Improvising a scene without using the letter S is one of my favourite improv games and one that I frequently use with the agile teams that I coach. So I wrote the preface entirely without using the letter S. At almost 900 words long, this was quite a challenge (for my editor as well as me!) but this constraint made that chapter one of the most interesting ones to write. Where I would have used a more common everyday word that I would type almost without thinking, I was forced to slow my typing speed and think more about the vocabulary and sentence structure, but still get my message across as cohesive prose.

The second part of the experiment was a question: given how important sensitivity is, would you as a reader be aware enough to spot the constraints I used?

PLAY

SENSITIVITY

GAMES

Sensitivity Games

The games in this chapter are designed to enhance and develop your sensitivity to both verbal and non-verbal cues.

BEEP BEEP[20]

Players	Timebox	Energy Level	Individual	Team	Visual	Verbal	Physical	Scenario
5–9	15 mins	***	****	***	*****	***	**	Daily Stand-up

Synopsis

One player must speak and hold the attention of the rest of the group by maintaining eye contact with every attendee. The listening players indicate engagement by holding up their hands; they lower their hands slowly as they become less engaged and then signal with an audible beep when the speaking player loses their attention completely.

Script

Arrange the group where one player is addressing the rest of the players, the audience. The audience should remain seated. If the speaker stands up, he or she will stand a better chance of keeping the audience's attention.

FACILITATOR [TO SPEAKER]: "You have to speak about your given subject for one minute. During that time you must remain engaged with each member of your audience."

FACILITATOR [TO AUDIENCE]: "Each of you needs to start the game with one hand raised above your head. As you feel less engaged with the speaker, drop your hand slowly towards your lap. When your hand hits your lap, make a beeping sound until the speaker re-engages with you.

At that point, return your hand back to its starting position and repeat the process."

Side Coaching

"Don't lose your audience! Get their attention!"

"Hold eye contact! Widen the eyes!"

Fleeting glances won't be enough to re-engage people – highlight the importance of making connections with fellow players.

Shift

After one minute, switch the speaker around with another player and repeat until everyone has played the speaker.

Speculation

"How did you keep the audience engaged?"

"When did you lose engagement?"

"What made the speaker engaging?"

"Was it easier or harder than you thought?"

Suggestions

Speaker emotions: in secret, ask the speaker to assume the audience has some affliction, such as:
- they smell awful;
- they are all very attractive; or
- they are aggressively hostile.

The trick is to not give away what the affliction is. During the debrief, talk about how the affliction affected the audience engagement.

LAST LETTER FIRST STAND-UP[21]

Players	Timebox	Energy Level	Individual	Team	Visual	Verbal	Physical	Scenario
5–9	15 mins	**	****	***	*	****	**	Daily Stand-up

Synopsis

In this circular speaking game, each player must give an update or make a speech that begins with the last letter used by the previous player. This encourages the team to listen to every word each player says.

Script

Arrange the players in a circle, preferably standing.

FACILITATOR: "We are going to give our updates today in random order, but each of you must start your update using the last letter that the previous player speaks. For instance, if I said, 'I bought some eggs today. Tomorrow I will a make an omelette,' then the next person must start with a word that begins with an *e*. For instance, 'Everyone we surveyed yesterday was happy with the cheese we chose for the omelette. Today I plan to source some tomatoes to go in it.' And so on."

Choose a player at random to start.

The game works best when the player selects who will carry on (usually by pointing at the chosen person) immediately after speaking.

Side Coaching

"If you can't think of a word, try using a person's name that begins with that letter!"

Speculation

"What senses were heightened by this game?"

"How was this different from other stand-ups you've attended in the past?"

Suggestions

Repeat as the ABC game, where each update must start with the next letter of the alphabet. This adds a memory test of remembering which letter should be coming next. Ask the players whether this variation increased or decreased their listening? Why?

COPYCAT[22]

Players	Timebox	Energy Level	Individual	Team	Visual	Verbal	Physical	Scenario
5–9	15 mins	***	****	***	*****	*	**	Anytime

Synopsis

In this mime game, players copy the actions of a leader while one "detective" tries to determine the player who is instigating the action. This increases observation skills in both the detective and the players who are following the leader.

Script

Players should stand in a circle, with the detective standing in the centre.

FACILITATOR: "The aim of this game is for the detective, the player standing in the centre, to work out who is controlling the rest of the group. While the detective isn't looking, I will choose one of you as the leader. The rest of you will be copycats. The leader will make small movements or gestures that the copycats must follow. The detective must try and work out who the leader of the copycats is. If you are discovered as the leader, you must confess. Then you become the detective and I will choose a new leader."

The facilitator then asks the detective to close his or her eyes. The facilitator then walks around the circle and touches the shoulder of the chosen leader. It is important that the copycats all see who the leader is, without giving it away to the detective.

Allow the detective to open his or her eyes and begin the game.

Side Coaching

"Subtle movements work best!"

"Don't give it away!"

"Watch the eyes…"

Shift

Once the leader is discovered, switch the detective with the leader, and repeat the process to select another leader in secret. Don't allow the detective to become overly frustrated. Should any detective struggle to identify the leader after a reasonable period of time, call a halt to the game, reveal the leader, and mix the roles once again.

Speculation

"What were you looking for as a copycat? As a detective?"

"What gave someone away?"

"Who was good at this game? Why?"

"How does this game benefit us?"

Suggestions

Experiment with an audio version of the game using sounds instead of mime. This will change the focus to listening skills.

DUBBING[23]

Players	Timebox	Energy Level	Individual	Team	Visual	Verbal	Physical	Scenario
4–16	15 mins	**	***	****	****	****	***	Anytime

Synopsis

The players mime a scene while the dialogue is added by two other players off stage. The offstage players have to observe the mime very carefully, while the onstage player listens for direction.

Script

Four players are needed for this game. It's useful to demonstrate first to any remaining players and then break off into smaller groups to try.

FACILITATOR: "You need to be in two pairs for this game. One person from each pair can only speak; the other person from each pair can only mime."

Allow the pairs to determine which role they want to play.

FACILITATOR: "The two mimes will meet on the centre of the stage and make something, which will be suggested by the listening players. The two speakers will remain off stage and provide the dialogue for their miming partners. You need to pay close attention to the mimes, and vice versa."

Take a suggestion from the listening players for a product or food item for the mimes to make.

Side Coaching

"Slow down. More obvious movements make this game easier for the speakers!"

Shift

Once the game is well understood, break larger groups into groups of four to try for themselves. Encourage the speakers and mimes to switch places after their scene completes.

Speculate

"What skills were you using there?"

"What made things clearer?"

"Who was influencing whom during that game?"

"Were you made to do something you didn't want to do? How did you react to that?"

Suggestions

This is not for the faint-hearted but you can try inserting a third pair of players into the scene – the amount of observing and listening must increase to match the increase in players.

ZIP ZAP ZOP[24]

Players	Timebox	Energy Level	Individual	Team	Visual	Verbal	Physical	Scenario
5–9	5 mins	***	****	*	***	*	***	Anytime

Synopsis

This is a simple game involving listening, observation, and memory. The players must simulate an electric bolt moving around the group by clapping their hands, shouting "Zip", "Zap", or "Zop" in sequence repeatedly, and then pointing to the next player.

Script

Players need to be standing in a circle with plenty of space around them.

FACILITATOR: "We are going to simulate electricity randomly moving through the group by shouting 'Zip!' 'Zap!' or 'Zop!' each time it touches one of us. To pass it on, you must clap your hands, shout the next word in the sequence, and then point to someone else, in one smooth and quick motion!"

FACILITATOR: "Try to make eye contact with the next person before you pass on the lightning bolt! The aim of the game is to try and get the electric bolt moving as quickly as we can."

Side Coaching

You may need to slow the game down at first until players become familiar with the game and find an initial rhythm. Failing the game is acceptable and part of the fun. Allow play to restart quickly so people don't dwell on it for too long.

The "Zip, Zap, Zop" sequence should repeat in order, and as players tune in, the speed of the game should increase.

Speculation

"How did you improve at the game?"

"What skills were you using?"

"What caused the game to break down?"

Suggestions

If anyone pauses or hesitates, ask that person to walk slowly around the outside of the circle as a forfeit while the game restarts. This makes the game harder for those left (fewer players) and adds change when that player re-enters.

For groups who relish the challenge, add a second electric bolt. Start the two together and keep a synchronised rhythm. This game is tough because the observation level takes a big step up.

Afterword:
THE COMEDY STORE
PLAYERS

"The Comedy Store Players is not an impro show.
It's a show about six people putting on an impro show."
Jim Sweeney, Improviser and Former Comedy Store Player[1]

The Comedy Store Players (from left to right): Andy Smart, Neil Mullarkey, Paul Merton, Richard Vranch, Josie Lawrence, and Lee Simpson

In October 1985, a young Canadian called Mike Myers (yes, that Mike Myers) brought together three other young comedians for the first improvisation performance at The Comedy Store in London's West End, under the banner of The Comedy Store Players.[3]

And now almost 30 years on, the players still have a regular slot at The Comedy Store, twice a week, and still manage to sell hundreds of tickets week in, week out. This legendary improv troupe has a place in the Guinness World Records as the world's longest-running comedy show with the same cast.[4]

Of course, during such a long period of time, players have come and gone. Myers flew back to the USA to become a regular on Saturday Night Live, on his way to Hollywood stardom as characters Wayne Campbell and Austin Powers. Several of The Comedy Store Players went on to appear as guests on a UK TV production called *Whose Line Is It Anyway?* This show brought improvisational theatre games to the masses in an entertaining and incredibly watchable format. The show was later brought to the attention of Drew Carey in the USA, who convinced the ABC network to sanction test episodes for a US audience, and before long, improv shows were becoming more mainstream entertainment.[5]

Whose Line Is It Anyway? was a TV show I can remember watching through my teenage years, and is probably where my interest and passion for improvisation started all those years ago. Little did I know that the same performers I used to watch and admire on television would agree to be interviewed as part of the research for this book, contributing invaluable quotes and background information. Many of the facts and quotes in this afterword come from my conversations with the following players: Neil Mullarkey, Richard Vranch, Andy Smart, and Lee Simpson.

Other than being the source for the distinct parallels between agile software development and improvisational theatre that I have described in this book, The Comedy Store Players piqued my interest as a good example of an established, high-performing, and self-organising team – a team tasked with delivering laughter and enjoyment to an audience through performance, as opposed to building and deploying software products through an agile process.

Team Size

I have spent many nights at The Comedy Store in recent years, watching these talented professional improvisers on stage. The team size for The Comedy Store Players is always set at six for a show. Why? The players I spoke to said that they have found that six players can all fit on The Comedy Store stage (just about), each player has an opportunity to rest between games, and the games they usually play work best for six players or fewer.

The team size of six is a given for The Comedy Store Players, but other UK-based improv troupes do vary in size. For example, Paul Merton's Impro Chums tour as a group of five improvisers, whereas Stephen Frost's Impro Allstars tour is only a four-piece group. Members of a smaller troupe will spend less time off stage, which can be more exhausting for the performers as they have to play a part in almost every game. Bigger troupes like The Comedy Store Players have more slack time to rest between games.[6] At the same time, if the team was any larger, the number of characters on stage would become confusing for the audience and the troupe would risk losing their attention and engagement. Not to mention the fact that the players could spend large amounts of time off stage, making it harder for them to stay "in the moment" with their teammates.

The same can be true of the team size of the agile teams I have worked with over the years. Too small and there is very little slack time built into their work, but too big and the team doesn't gel as well. A team of between five and seven members seems to be the right size as no one gets exhausted, plus the team can lose a team member to illness for a large percentage of the iteration and probably still be able to pick up the slack and complete their commitment.

A Family Affair

*"I feel more comfortable on that stage sometimes than
I do in my living room. That stage is my living room."*
Andy Smart [7]

What intrigued me about The Comedy Store Players is their secret to
longevity, a secret that has kept them together since 1985. The players
I spoke to all agreed that part of the reason they all stick together is the
joy of improvising, the thrill of spontaneity, and their comfort with being
on a stage, an element missing from recorded television work. But these
elements are only part of the story. The players explained that the core
group's bonds are akin to that of a family. Some of the current crop of
players have been performing together for over 25 years. During that
time they have aged together almost as siblings, and have watched their
dynamic change over time. After early shows they would enjoy a meal
together before then drinking long into the night and ending up in
a nightclub in an odd part of London somewhere. But now, they tend
to perform on stage and then go their own separate ways until the next
performance, not because their bonds are weaker but because they have
simply grown up. [8]

Many of the group's current players have many other roles and
opportunities beyond The Comedy Store. Paul Merton and Josie
Lawrence are still heavily involved in television and radio work, while
Neil Mullarkey has moved into coaching and educating business
professionals in improvisational skills away from the stage. Andy Smart
and Richard Vranch still spend time on the road touring with other
improv groups, performing for audiences all over the world.

Yet the family still comes home twice a week to entertain The Comedy
Store crowd – and to make each other laugh as well. The bond within the
group has been strong enough to help some of the players through their
own personal difficulties. The group describes it as "therapeutic". [9]

But as with most close family relationships, there have been (and
continue to be) niggles, fall-outs, and feuds. The players I spoke to openly

admit that it's not always one big happy family. The players acknowledge that they may have picked up bad habits or quirks that other players would prefer them not to do (as all families do) but there is a tacit acceptance of those foibles and individual styles.

> *"We drive each other crazy. We will get angry with each other in the dressing room, and we will get angry with each other on stage."*
> Lee Simpson[10]

Well-formed, long-lived agile development teams I have worked with develop a similar family dynamic over time, with the same highs and lows. I firmly believe healthy conflict can be a positive energy. It shows a degree of passion, gives a team an identity, acts as a defence mechanism, and prevents groupthink by really challenging the group into not accepting the first idea that comes to them. When individuals are part of an agile team, they have to trust each other enough to allow conflict and passion to come through, without becoming destructive to the group or getting too personal.

I have always said that you can tell if team bonds have become strong if team members can enjoy being in a social atmosphere together. The Comedy Store Players went through that forming process many years ago.

> *"As a group of improvisers we have always socialized well together. You become friends with the people you regularly improvise with, and the good feeling you engender onstage carries over into real life."*
> Paul Merton[11]

I worked with an agile team once who had seconded a university student for a full year during his "year in industry", standard policy for this particular company. While some students never really adopt the company values or embrace the industry experience, for one student, Stuart, working on an agile team was instrumental in becoming part of a mature team. When Stuart's year came to an end, his final retrospective was littered with sticky notes from his fellow teammates, who were genuinely sad he was ending his time with the team. They felt they were losing a friend as well as a team member. This is just one example I have seen of where an agile process was instrumental in welcoming new team members, and forging stronger bonds than the team thought possible.

Generalising Specialists

Agile development teams strive for a spread of skills and functions across team members. While this is sometimes difficult to achieve in the early stages of team formation, the long-term benefits come in the form of a team that can more effectively swarm around the higher priority work in the backlog, or a team that can reduce their own bottlenecks and increase their flow of work achieved. These types of team members are sometimes referred to as generalising specialists. These team members have a great talent in a particular function or skill, but are comfortable and prepared enough to take on some other function (when required), allowing the team to alleviate a blocked task or swarm over a difficult or time-consuming task.

To my surprise, most improv troupes I have seen are no different. While some of the functions are more blatant to the audience, others are a little more subtle to the untrained eye.

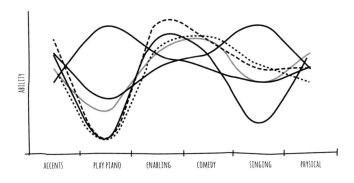

Figure A.1 Examples of the spread of skills across an improv troupe

Within The Comedy Store Players, the players themselves are very aware of their own strengths and weaknesses and the other players on stage will (usually) respect those and play within them. For example, Josie Lawrence is an extremely talented singer. And the group will look to Josie to take the lead on sung improv scenes and carry some of the other players along with her. Neil Mullarkey, by his own admission, does not enjoy singing so the players (usually) respect that too.[12] Equally, the players know that Andy Smart cannot imitate a good Russian accent, while Lee Simpson excels at almost any accent.[13]

Some of the more subtle skills that are harder to spot on stage are leading and enabling. Leading a scene helps keep the story flowing and interesting to the audience by moving on at the appropriate point. Enabling other performers on stage allows others to appear funny to the members of the audience (making them look good!).

However, in some situations (such as a musical version of an improvised story) certain players may be caught on stage and have to sing, even when they'd prefer not to. The other players know that and try to rescue them when they can. And sometimes watching the less able generalist is more entertaining for the audience than watching the more able specialist – as the audience almost wants them to struggle and fail!

The responsibility of scheduling the six performers appearing on any given night is rotated between Neil (Mullarkey), Richard (Vranch), Lee (Simpson), and Andy (Smart) each month.[14] Each show will always require a musician who can play the piano for the musical games. But once that requirement has been filled, the standard of the players is sufficiently high and all are adaptable enough that scheduling the performers is relatively simple compared to resourcing a new software development team dependent on a cross-section of skills. Despite strengths and weaknesses, all performers are competent in improvisational comedy, but each one brings a unique personal style to the table.

In the group's infancy, the improvisational experience came from across the Atlantic in the form of two talented North American performers, Kit Hollerbach and Mike Myers. Kit and Mike passed on the ethos of improvisation to the new British performers in the group.[15]

The gulf in improvisational ability was daunting to the less experienced players in those early days, especially when Mike (Myers) was on stage. So much so that they only really showed signs of improvement when Mike returned to the USA.[16]

"When Mike [Myers] was with us in the early days, he was so good, he could go on and be better than us at any game. It was only when he temporarily went over to Second City [Toronto] that we had to step up and do those things which Mike did so well."
Richard Vranch[17]

The same is true of my experience when coaching agile teams. Senior team members are usually more comfortable and skilled enough to take on tasks or activities that the iteration demands. This makes more junior team members feel comfortable in the knowledge that the difficult or challenging tasks will be picked up by their more senior colleagues.

I was one of those junior developers in my first team back in 2001. I worked with the senior Java developer in the team, Pete. I can still remember the panic that hit me when Pete told me he had quit. Who would do the deployments? How should we package the release? These were all duties that I had relied on Pete to do without question, but now he wouldn't be around and I would need to make these decisions and learn some of his skills. While daunting, this turned out to be a catalyst for me to improve my own knowledge of the system and the deployment procedures, and ultimately increase my own skill as a developer.

Playful Misbehaviour

A "code of conduct" is a great way for any team to establish a common foundation to build upon, and The Comedy Store Players are no exception. They follow simple rules to ensure the performances run smoothly, and the audience and players are safe in their environment. Firstly, all the players are expected to arrive no later than 35 minutes before the show commences.[18]

Each player is left to prepare in his or her own way before going on stage. Some will do a crossword, some will check email, some will chat about what they did that day, but the players always come together to run through a version of the Die storytelling game (see Chapter 3, "Storytelling"), in the privacy of the dressing room, as final preparation before the curtain goes up.[19] They also follow the credo of alternative comedy: no sexism, no racism, and no homophobia.[20] This applies not only to the players themselves, but also as a way of screening inappropriate suggestions from an overly exuberant audience.

A by-product of The Comedy Store Players' rapport with each other on stage is their tendency to misbehave on or off stage. While this sounds detrimental to a good performance, this is what makes The Comedy Store Players so joyful to watch, and also makes them appear more human to members of the audience.

> *"It's because we know the rules that we can break them.*
> *You have to know the rules before you can go that far out.*
> *And it's about knowing each other's strengths..."*
> Andy Smart[21]

The players will blatantly tease each other on stage by grabbing body parts, name-calling, or by cleverly using complex words that they know certain players won't understand! This might not strictly fit improv author and educator Keith Johnstone's definition of great improv but it does provide a certain "crackle".[22]

The best agile teams I work with are those who have also established ground rules for how they work and established a certain level of trust and rapport between their members. Once those rules become embedded and understood, those teams can benefit from more enhanced collaboration both inside and occasionally (and respectfully) outside of those rules.

Essential Guests

> *"It's not often we have new people. That's not because we are against it; in fact, we actively want to have new people when the guest slots become available because we think it keeps us fresh."*
> Richard Vranch[23]

As it's The Comedy Store Players themselves who schedule the improvisers for any given night, it's quite possible the regular six performers may not all be able to perform due to conflicting schedules. So in light of this, and in the interests of keeping the team young and fresh, they will occasionally invite other improvisers to guest with them. Interestingly, the players I spoke to view this as a way to improve their own awareness and performance, by removing bad habits that the "family" may have picked up over time.

> *"If it was just the six of us, and we had no guests coming in, we'd have collapsed because just having the same six people in every show gets stale. Having guests coming in with their own energy, stories, dress sense, and sense of humour – that little bit of variety is what actually keeps it going."*
> Richard Vranch[24]

In my experience, new team members in agile development teams are expected to play by the team's existing rules. My suggestion, however, is to take these new member introductions as a great opportunity to review the existing team norms and rules, and make some adjustments to ensure the new team member can "play" effectively.

Coincidently, The Comedy Store Players do a similar thing. The existing players flex to accommodate the contrasting style that a new improviser can bring.[25]

> *"We are very good at making them [the guest] relaxed and supporting them. It is a supportive mechanism once we go on stage."*
> Richard Vranch[26]

Guest performers who I have seen work well with The Comedy Store Players include Stephen Frost, Steve Steen, and Niall Ashdown. Surprisingly though, some of the more famous names in improv have appeared with the players but have not been asked back.

"Some people have been good, but very nervous in the dressing room. And you don't need that before you go out on stage. The atmosphere in the dressing room is quite important before a show. There are very few comics that we can invite down that can actually just walk straight in and do it. There are some acts we have had down who crave the audience's attention too much, and they don't get asked back."
Andy Smart[27]

A question I get asked a lot is "How should an agile team deal with a dysfunctional member of the team?" I have seen a few examples of team members who are negatively affecting a team's performance, morale, and ability to collaborate. Often this is due to a difference in personality or a lack of respect for the team values or the other members themselves. My advice to these teams is usually quite blunt – the team itself should feel empowered enough to remove their own impediments to being productive, and sometimes those impediments could be team members. Most teams I have worked with would give those new or difficult team members a few chances to redeem themselves and even adjust to their needs and values if possible. But inevitably if the team member doesn't fit the team, the team member shouldn't be in the team – the same policy The Comedy Store Players follow with their guest performers.

Customer Collaboration

Improvisational comedy thrives on an audience's suggestions, so when you buy a ticket to watch The Comedy Store Players, you, as the paying customer, feel like you are part of their games. The players respond to the audience, and vice versa, in a two-way collaboration. Accepting suggestions from an audience is an extremely brave act. There are no good or bad suggestions. Of course, some could be wholly inappropriate or distasteful, which the players and indeed the groaning audience would reject. But the players largely accept anything the audience throws at them. They are able to make an innocuous object or location into an entertaining scene. This makes the audience feel part of the performance and that they have contributed to the success of the show that night.

This warm glow is the same feeling that members of an agile team should feel when they are collaborating effectively with their own customers. Taking the suggestions on board from stakeholders makes everyone feel part of the product delivery.

In one of the first Scrum projects I worked on in BT, we were developing queuing software for call centres that would allow the staff to see which accounts had been allocated to them for that day. As a ScrumMaster of that team, I arranged for the developers to visit one of the call centres to see the product they built being used, but mainly to meet the staff who use it and build relationships with them. Over time (and regular visits) the team developed empathy and rapport with the staff members using the software. It was a positive, collaborative experience for both parties. When a new feature was suggested or added, both parties felt like they had been part of its discovery and implementation.

Secrets to Success

So what is the secret to the players' success and longevity? "Money, of course!" replies Andy Smart flippantly when I pose this question to him.[28] While The Comedy Store still reigns as the most famous and popular comedy venue in London and will regularly pull audiences of 350 or more,[29] even Andy agreed that there is more to their sustained act than just the income it provides.[30]

> *"We do enjoy it…"*
> Lee Simpson[31]

Paul Merton describes the weekly improvising as a great way to hone skills and remain sharp as a comedy performer.[32] The variety of the suggestions means that no two shows are ever the same. But most of all I think the players keep coming back to perform because they enjoy performing together, as a group of friends they trust and enjoy working with. The best agile teams I have worked with would cite the same reasons.

The onstage rapport that has developed over the years makes this group one of the most watchable comedy acts currently on stage in London. Each of the performers is willing to show his or her weaknesses on stage as well as his or her strengths. They play within their games, and they play beyond their games. They poke fun at each other and they laugh at each other's misgivings. This closeness and "crackle" that Lee Simpson describes[33] is what still draws me back to The Comedy Store whenever I crave an evening of merriment in the West End of London.

You can catch The Comedy Store Players in London every Wednesday and Sunday evening. You can read more details at www.comedystoreplayers.com.

Appendix:
THE APPLIED
IMPROVISATION
NETWORK

The fundamentals of improvisational theatre are as useful to us in everyday life as they are on the stage. One person who knows this very well is consultant, trainer, and author Paul Z. Jackson.[1] In a December 2014 interview with Jackson, I learned more about his background and the community he co-founded in order to create and share experiences of applying improvisation in work and life.

In 1992 Jackson began studying and practising improvisation with improv troupes across the United Kingdom. Over the next ten years, he used the improvisational skills and games he had learned from the theatre to teach organisational development and run training courses. He taught corporate leaders how to think on their feet, deal with uncertainty, and develop their presentation skills.

Successful but a bit isolated, Jackson attended a conference in Florida where he discovered two other trainers who were also using improvisational techniques in their training. Together, they formed the Applied Improvisation Network (AIN).[2] The purpose of the community is to share ideas and experiences where the principles of improvisational theatre have been applied in a variety of contexts. Applications shared by this group range from delivering improvisational classes at Apple, all the way through to providing disaster relief in the Philippines.[3]

What started as a simple mailing list in 2002 between just three people has now grown into a global community supported by over 5,000 members. This community stays active thanks to regular social gatherings and meet-ups, and an international conference once every year.[4]

As a member of this community myself, I am always learning from a wealth of information and ideas within this community. If applying improvisation interests you, I can guarantee you will find this group has a lot to offer those who are involved with making agile software development a success in their companies.

You can get involved with the AIN at www.appliedimprov.com.

Index of
GAMES AND
TECHNIQUES

This book contains many different ways that you can start to understand the nature of improvisation and how to apply it within an agile context. This matrix lists all of the games and exercises in this book and their corresponding chapter names. The chapter names also reflect the purpose and intent of each game or exercise.

Some of the games might be described in one chapter but could also help teams and individuals practise other skills, which is why you will see some games attached to more than one chapter name.

Games with detailed instructions at the end of each chapter are marked in **bold**.

	Page number	Safety	Spontaneity	Storytelling	Status	Sensitivity
Five-Word Goals	76			•		
Goldfish Bowl	96		•	•		
I Am a Tree	58		•			•
I Quit… Dumbass!	130	•			•	
Identifying Status	107				•	
Last Letter First Stand-up	158		•			•
Link the Items	98		•	•		
Mad, Bad, Stupid	42		•			
Mime Stand-up	144		•			•
Not Advancing	18	•				•
One Failure, Five Positives	10	•				
One Voice	28	•				
One-Word Stand-up	63		•	•		
Psychic Stand-up	32	•				•
Selfless Act	138					•
Share Your Struggle	7	•				
Simplify the Task	77			•		
Slow Your Mind	16	•				
Smelly, Sexy, Stupid	128				•	
Spot the Offers	47		•			
Status Corridor	124				•	
Status Match	112				•	•
Status Stand-up	126				•	
Story Spines	100			•		
Swedish Story	90		•	•		
The Dinner Party	122				•	
The Status Chair	110				•	
Toothless Stand-up	141					•
Trying Too Hard	13	•				
Wear the Hat	44		•			
What's in the Box?	64		•			
Word-At-A-Time Storytelling	94		•	•		
Words to Remember	147			•		•
Yes, And	50		•			
Yes, But	48		•			
Zip Zap Zop	164					•

NOTES

NOTES TO FOREWORD BY NEIL MULLARKEY

1. Rainer Maria Rilke, goodreads.com, http://www.goodreads.com/quotes/ 717-be-patient-toward-all-that-is-unsolved-in-your-heart (accessed 4 June 2015).

NOTES TO PREFACE

1. Wikipedia contributors, "Viola Spolin", *Wikipedia, The Free Encyclopedia*, http://en.wikipedia.org/w/index.php?title=Viola_Spolin&oldid=660653940 (accessed 3 June 2015).

2. Wikipedia contributors, "List of alumni of the Second City", *Wikipedia, The Free Encyclopedia*, http://en.wikipedia.org/w/index.php?title=List_of_alumni_of_the_ Second_City&oldid=665208071 (accessed 3 June 2015).

NOTES TO CHAPTER 1, "SAFETY"

1. Patrick Lencioni, *The Five Dysfunctions of a Team* (San Francisco: Jossey-Bass, 2002).

2. Richard Vranch, in interview with author, 23 October 2014.

3. Thomas Edison, BrainyQuote.com, http://www.brainyquote.com/quotes/quotes/t/ thomasaed132683.html (accessed 30 April 2015).

4. Hammad Latif, "10 Inventions That Were Created Accidentally", Galakcious, under "Interesting", http://galakcious.blogspot.co.uk/2014/04/10-inventions-that-were-created-accidentally.html (accessed 30 April 2015).

5. Ken Robinson, "How Schools Kill Creativity", Ted Talk at *Ted2006*, filmed February 2006, http://www.ted.com/talks/ken_robinson_says_schools_kill_creativity?language=en (accessed 30 April 2015).

6. Andy Smart, from interview with author, 10 September 2014.

7. Richard Vranch, in interview with author, 23 October 2014.

8. Andy McCann, from seminar "The Coach and the Entrepreneur", Bath, 2 September 2014.

9. Wikipedia contributors, "Flow (psychology)", *Wikipedia, The Free Encyclopedia*, http://en.wikipedia.org/w/index.php?title=Flow_(psychology)&oldid=663423171 (accessed 3 June 2015).

10. Keith Johnstone, from workshop "Keith in London 2014", London, 8 September 2014.

11. Mike Cohn, "My Primary Criticism of Scrum", Mountain Goat Software, 22 July 2014, http://www.mountaingoatsoftware.com/blog/my-primary-criticism-of-scrum (accessed 29 April 2015).

12. Ken Schwaber and Mike Beedle, *Agile Software Development with Scrum* (Prentice Hall, 2001).

13. Albert Einstein, BrainyQuote.com, http://www.brainyquote.com/quotes/authors/a/albert_einstein.html (accessed 30 April 2015).

14. Guy Claxton, *Hare Brain, Tortoise Mind* (Fourth Estate Ltd, 1998).

15. Keith Johnstone, from workshop "Keith in London 2014", London, 8 September 2014.

16. Charlie Chaplin, *City Lights*, YouTube, 5:00, https://www.youtube.com/watch?v=UkDf5dYmkaY (accessed 15 January 2014).

17. Paul Z. Jackson, revised game from workshop "Improvisation at Work", London, 15–16 March 2014.

18. Keith Johnstone, based on game from *Impro for Storytellers* (London: Faber & Faber, 1999).

19. Keith Johnstone, based on game from *Impro for Storytellers* (London: Faber & Faber, 1999).

20. Paul Z. Jackson, revised game from workshop "Improvisation at Work", London, 15–16 March 2014.

NOTES TO CHAPTER 2, "SPONTANEITY"

1. Jennifer Aniston, BrainyQuote.com, http://www.brainyquote.com/quotes/quotes/j/jenniferan470473.html (accessed 21 May 2015).

2. Kent Beck et al., "Manifesto for Agile Software Development", AgileManifesto.org, http://www.agilemanifesto.org (accessed 6 May 2015).

3. Spontaneous, Google definition, https://www.google.com/#q=spontaneous (accessed 21 May 2015).

4. Kent Beck et al., "Manifesto for Agile Software Development", AgileManifesto.org, http://www.agilemanifesto.org (accessed 6 May 2015).

5. Keith Johnstone, *Impro: Improvisation and the Theatre* (Bloomsbury Methuen Drama, 2007).

6. Charlie Chaplin, "Keith in London 2014", Quote relayed in workshop by Keith Johnstone, London, 8 September 2014.

7. Pamela Hutchinson, "Charlie Chaplin and the Tramp: The Birth of a Hero", *The Guardian* online, Film Blog, 27 January 2014, http://www.theguardian.com/film/filmblog/2014/jan/27/charlie-chaplin-tramp-birth-hero (accessed 6 May 2015).

8. Wikipedia contributors, "Six Thinking Hats", *Wikipedia, The Free Encyclopedia*, http://en.wikipedia.org/w/index.php?title=Six_Thinking_Hats&oldid=646303838 (accessed 3 June 2015).

9. Neil Mullarkey, "Collaborate to Create", TedX Youth@Bath, 5 December 2011, http://youtu.be/grVAFzmCvn4 (accessed 6 May 2015).

10. Sue Walden, "Applied Improv Session on Empowerment: Another Application of 'Yes, And'", Meetup.com, 8 May 2012, http://www.meetup.com/Applied-Improvisation-London/events/55875002/ (accessed 6 May 2015).

11. Richard Vranch, in interview with author, 23 October 2014.

12. Henrik Kniberg and Anders Ivarsson, "Scaling Agile @Spotify with Tribes, Squads, Chapters & Guilds", October 2012, https://dl.dropboxusercontent.com/u/1018963/Articles/SpotifyScaling.pdf (accessed 6 May 2015).

13. Paul Z. Jackson, revised game from workshop "Improvisation at Work", London, 15–16 March 2014.

14. Keith Johnstone, revised game from workshop "Keith in London 2014", London, 8 September 2014.

15. Keith Johnstone, revised game from *Impro: Improvisation and the Theatre* (Bloomsbury Methuen Drama, 2007).

16. Paul Z. Jackson, revised game from *58½ Ways To Improvise In Training* (Crown House Publishing Ltd., 2003).

17. Neil Mullarkey, revised game from workshop "Creative Collaboration", London, 21 June 2012.

NOTES TO CHAPTER 3, "STORYTELLING"

1. Story, definition from Merriam-Webster.com, http://www.merriam-webster.com/dictionary/story (accessed 29 May 2015).

2. Leo Widrich, "Science of Storytelling: What Listening to a Story Does to Our Brains", BufferApp.com, Buffer Social Blog, 29 November 2012, https://blog.bufferapp.com/science-of-storytelling-why-telling-a-story-is-the-most-powerful-way-to-activate-our-brains (accessed 29 May 2015).

3. Annie M. Paul, "Your Brain on Fiction", *New York Times* online, Sunday Review, Opinion, 17 March 2012, http://www.nytimes.com/2012/03/18/opinion/sunday/the-neuroscience-of-your-brain-on-fiction.html?pagewanted=all&_r=0 (accessed 29 May 2015).

4. Wikipedia contributors, "Hook (filmmaking)", *Wikipedia, The Free Encyclopedia*, http://en.wikipedia.org/w/index.php?title=Hook_(filmmaking)&oldid=609502444 (accessed June 3, 2015).

5. Keith Johnstone, *Impro: Improvisation and the Theatre* (Bloomsbury Methuen Drama, 2007).

6. Kent Beck et al., "Manifesto for Agile Software Development", AgileManifesto.org, http://www.agilemanifesto.org (accessed 6 May 2015).

7. Steve Jobs, Goodreads.com, http://www.goodreads.com/quotes/445279-simple-can-be-harder-than-complex-you-have-to-work (accessed 29 May 2015).

8. Boris Gloger, "Ball Point Game: Feel the Scrum Flow", borisgloger.com,http://borisgloger.com/wp-content/uploads/2011/08/Ball_Point_Game.pdf?882268 (accessed 29 May 2015).

9. Emma Coats, "22 #Storybasics I've Picked Up in My Time at Pixar", Tumblr Blog StoryShots, http://storyshots.tumblr.com/post/25032057278/22-storybasics-ive-picked-up-in-my-time-at-pixar (accessed 29 May 2015).

10. Wikipedia contributors, "Persona (user experience)", *Wikipedia, The Free Encyclopedia*, http://en.wikipedia.org/w/index.php?title=Persona_(user_experience)&oldid=664055497 (accessed 3 June 2015).

11. Emma Coats, "22 #Storybasics I've Picked Up in My Time at Pixar", Tumblr Blog StoryShots, http://storyshots.tumblr.com/post/25032057278/22-storybasics-ive-picked-up-in-my-time-at-pixar (accessed 29 May 2015).

12. Neil Mullarkey, revised game from workshop "Creative Collaboration", London, 21 June 2012.

13. Keith Johnstone, based on game from *Impro for Storytellers* (London: Faber & Faber, 1999).

14. Neil Mullarkey, revised game from workshop "Creative Collaboration", London, 21 June 2012.

15. Keith Johnstone, based on game from *Impro for Storytellers* (London: Faber & Faber, 1999).

16. Kenn Adams, *How to Improvise a Full-Length Play: The Art of Spontaneous Theater* (Allworth Press, 2007).

17. Kenn Adams, "Back to the Story Spine", Aerogramme Writers' Studio, 5 June 2013, http://www.aerogrammestudio.com/2013/06/05/back-to-the-story-spine/ (accessed 29 May 2015).

NOTES TO CHAPTER 4, "STATUS"

1. Keith Johnstone, *Impro: Improvisation and the Theatre* (Bloomsbury Methuen Drama, 2007).

2. Status, Merriam-Webster online, http://www.merriam-webster.com/dictionary/status (accessed 19 November 2014).

3. Brett Johnson, "7 Great Keith Johnstone Quotes on Improv and Performance", Comedy Conjectures, 12 February 2011, http://comedyconjectures.blogspot.com/2011/02/7-stellar-keith-johnstone-quotes-on.html (accessed 29 April 2015).

4. Keith Johnstone, "Keith in London 2014", Quotes from workshop by Keith Johnstone, London, 8 September 2014.

5. Dana R. Carney, Amy J.C. Cuddy, and Andy J. Yap, "Power Posing: Brief Nonverbal Displays Affect Neuroendocrine Levels and Risk Tolerance", *Psychological Science*, Online, 21 September 2010, http://pss.sagepub.com/content/21/10/1363.short (accessed 29 May 2015).

6. Kent Beck et al., "Manifesto for Agile Software Development", AgileManifesto.org, http://www.agilemanifesto.org (accessed 6 May 2015).

7. Wikipedia contributors, "Mirroring (psychology)", *Wikipedia, The Free Encyclopedia*, http://en.wikipedia.org/w/index.php?title=Mirroring_(psychology)&oldid=661597270 (accessed 3 June 2015).

8. Keith Johnstone, *Impro: Improvisation and the Theatre* (Bloomsbury Methuen Drama, 2007).

9. ibid.

10. Keith Johnstone, revised game from workshop "Keith in London 2014", London, 8 September 2014.
11. Neil Mullarkey, revised game from workshop "Creative Collaboration", London, 21 June 2012.
12. Keith Johnstone, based on game from *Impro for Storytellers* (London: Faber & Faber, 1999).

NOTES TO CHAPTER 5, "SENSITIVITY"

1. Sensitivity, Google definition, https://www.google.com/#q=sensitivity+definition (accessed 29 May 2015).
2. Bruce Lee, BrainyQuote.com, http://www.brainyquote.com/quotes/quotes/b/brucelee379710.html (accessed 29 May 2015).
3. Keith Johnstone, from workshop "Keith in London 2014", London, 8 September 2014.
4. Richard Sheridan, "The Business Value of Joy", End Keynote, Global Scrum Gathering New Orleans, 7 May 2014.
5. Jimmy Fallon, BrainyQuote.com, http://www.brainyquote.com/quotes/quotes/j/jimmyfallo364833.html (accessed 29 May 2015).
6. Julie Starr, *The Coaching Manual* (Prentice Hall, 2002).
7. Kent Beck et al., "Manifesto for Agile Software Development", AgileManifesto.org, http://www.agilemanifesto.org (accessed 6 May 2015).
8. Richard Vranch, in interview with author, 23 October 2014.
9. Guy Claxton, *Hare Brain, Tortoise Mind* (Fourth Estate Ltd, 1998).
10. Mark Bailey, "Sports Visualisation: How to Imagine Your Way to Success", *The Telegraph* online, Men, Active, 22 January 2014, http://www.telegraph.co.uk/men/active/10568898/Sports-visualisation-how-to-imagine-your-way-to-success.html (accessed 29 May 2015).
11. Keith Johnstone, *Impro for Storytellers* (London: Faber & Faber, 1999).
12. "How to Improve Your Memory", BBC One, Science and Nature: TV and Radio Follow-Up, 9 August 2006, http://www.bbc.co.uk/sn/tvradio/programmes/memory/programme.shtml (accessed 29 May 2015).
13. "Tips and Techniques to Improve Your Memory", BBC Radio 4, The Memory Experience: A Journey of Self Discovery, http://www.bbc.co.uk/radio4/memory/improve/ (accessed 29 May 2015).
14. "How to Improve Your Memory", BBC One, Science and Nature: TV and Radio Follow-Up, 9 August 2006, http://www.bbc.co.uk/sn/tvradio/programmes/memory/programme.shtml (accessed 29 May 2015).
15. Wikipedia contributors, "Emotional intelligence", *Wikipedia, The Free Encyclopedia*, http://en.wikipedia.org/w/index.php?title=Emotional_intelligence&oldid=664696329 (accessed 4 June 2015).

16. Bill Wake, "Scrum From Hell", xp123.com, http://xp123.com/articles/scrum-from-hell/ (accessed 4 June 2015).

17. Lee Simpson, in interview with author, 10 September 2014.

18. "Top Ten Improvised Movie Moments", WatchMojo.com, https://youtu.be/So9iCqdfUF4 (accessed 29 May 2015).

19. ibid.

20. Keith Johnstone, based on game from *Impro for Storytellers* (London: Faber & Faber, 1999).

21. Neil Mullarkey, revised game from workshop "Creative Collaboration", London, 21 June 2012.

22. Paul Z. Jackson, revised game from *58½ Ways To Improvise In Training* (Crown House Publishing Ltd., 2003).

23. ibid.

24. Paul Tevis, Global Scrum Gathering New Orleans, 5–7 May 2014.

NOTES TO AFTERWORD

1. Richard Vranch relayed this quote in an interview with author, 23 October 2014.

2. Comedy Store Players Image, comedystoreplayers.com, http://www.comedystoreplayers.com/ (accessed 4 June 2015).

3. Marc Maron, WTF with Marc Maron, "Episode 518: Mike Myers", 28 July 2014, http://www.wtfpod.com/podcast/episodes/episode_518_-_mike_myers (accessed 29 May 2015).

4. *Chortle*, "Long Players: Comedy Store Improvisers Get into the Record Books", http://www.chortle.co.uk/news/2010/11/01/12050/long_players (accessed 30 May 2015).

5. Wikipedia contributors, "Whose Line Is It Anyway? (UK TV series)", *Wikipedia, The Free Encyclopedia*, http://en.wikipedia.org/w/index.php?title=Whose_Line_Is_It_Anyway%3F_(UK_TV_series)&oldid=665198395 (accessed 4 June 2015).

6. Richard Vranch, in interview with author, 23 October 2014.

7. Andy Smart, in interview with author, 10 September 2014.

8. Lee Simpson, in interview with author, 10 September 2014.

9. Paul Merton, *Only When I Laugh* (Ebury Press, 2014).

10. Lee Simpson, in interview with author, 10 September 2014.

11. Paul Merton, *Only When I Laugh* (Ebury Press, 2014).

12. Neil Mullarkey, in interview with author, 17 September 2014.

13. Andy Smart, in interview with author, 10 September 2014.

14. Richard Vranch, in interview with author, 23 October 2014.

15. Marc Maron, WTF with Marc Maron, "Episode 518: Mike Myers", 28 July 2014, http://www.wtfpod.com/podcast/episodes/episode_518_-_mike_myers (accessed 29 May 2015).

16. Richard Vranch, in interview with author, 23 October 2014.
17. ibid.
18. Neil Mullarkey, in interview with author, 17 September 2014.
19. Lee Simpson, in interview with author, 10 September 2014.
20. Andy Smart, in interview with author, 10 September 2014.
21. ibid.
22. Lee Simpson, in interview with author, 10 September 2014.
23. Richard Vranch, in interview with author, 23 October 2014.
24. ibid.
25. Neil Mullarkey, in interview with author, 17 September 2014.
26. Richard Vranch, in interview with author, 23 October 2014.
27. Andy Smart, in interview with author, 10 September 2014.
28. ibid.
29. Lee Simpson, in interview with author, 10 September 2014.
30. Andy Smart, in interview with author, 10 September 2014.
31. Lee Simpson, in interview with author, 10 September 2014.
32. Paul Merton, *Only When I Laugh* (Ebury Press, 2014).
33. Lee Simpson, in interview with author, 10 September 2014.

NOTES TO APPENDIX

1. Paul Z. Jackson, Paul Jackson Associates, http://www.impro.org.uk (accessed 30 May 2015).
2. Paul Z. Jackson, in interview with author, 15 December 2014.
3. Applied Improvisation Network, http://www.appliedimprov.com (accessed 30 May 2015).
4. Paul Z. Jackson, in interview with author, 15 December 2014.

ADDITIONAL WORKS CONSULTED

Beck, Kent and Martin Fowler. 2000. *Planning Extreme Programming.* Addison Wesley.

Bugaj, Stephan V. 2013. *Pixar's 22 Rules of Story (That Aren't Really Pixar's).* The Sticking Place.com, http://www.thestickingplace.com/wp-content/uploads/2014/12/Pixars-22-Rules-of-Story-Bugaj.pdf (accessed 29 May 2015).

Cleese, John. *How to Be Creative.* Video Arts, 1991; 36 min., http://vimeo.com/89936101 (accessed 30 April 2015).

Goddard, Paul. 2011. "The Hook", Agilify, 30 March 2011, http://www.agilify.co.uk/agile-blog/hook (accessed 29 May 2015).

Improv Encyclopedia. "5 Basic Improv Rules", http://improvencyclopedia.org/references/5_Basic_Improv_Rules.html (accessed 30 April 2015).

Mayer, John D. "The Four Branch Model of Emotional Intelligence", UNH.edu, http://www.unh.edu/emotional_intelligence/ei%20What%20is%20EI/ei%20fourbranch.htm (accessed 29 May 2015).

Mayer, John D. "What Is Emotional Intelligence?", UNH.edu, http://www.unh.edu/emotional_intelligence/EI%20Assets/Reprints...EI%20Proper/EI1997MSWhatIsEI.pdf (accessed 29 May 2015).

Poppendieck, Mary and Tom Poppendieck. 2003. *Lean Software Development: An Agile Toolkit.* Addison Wesley.

Spolin, Viola. 1986. *Theatre Games for the Classroom.* Northwestern University Press.

Watts, Geoff. 2013. *ScrumMastery: From Good to Great Servant Leadership.* Inspect & Adapt Ltd.

West, Kristi. 2014. "Who's Afraid of the Big Bad Wolf: How to Manage Fear in the Workplace", The Brink Improv, 1 December 2014, http://www.thebrinkimprov.com/blog/2015/1/13/whos-afraid-of-the-big-bad-wolf-how-to-manage-fear-in-the-workplace (accessed 30 April 2015).